Loving Water across Religions

Ecology and Justice

An Orbis Series on Integral Ecology

Advisory Board Members
Mary Evelyn Tucker
John A. Grim
Leonardo Boff
Sean McDonagh

The Orbis Series on Integral Ecology publishes books seeking to integrate an understanding of Earth's interconnected life systems with sustainable social, political, and economic systems that enhance the Earth community. Books in the series concentrate on ways to:

- reexamine human–Earth relations in light of contemporary cosmological and ecological science
- develop visions of common life marked by ecological integrity and social justice
- expand on the work of those exploring such fields as integral ecology, climate justice, Earth law, eco-feminism, and animal protection
- promote inclusive participatory strategies that enhance the struggle of Earth's poor and oppressed for ecological justice
- deepen appreciation for dialogue within and among religious traditions on issues of ecology and justice
- encourage spiritual discipline, social engagement, and the transformation of religion and society towards these ends

Viewing the present moment as a time for fresh creativity and inspired by the encyclical *Laudato Si'*, the series seeks authors who speak to eco-justice concerns and who bring into this dialogue perspectives from the Christian communities, from the world's religions, from secular and scientific circles, or from new paradigms of thought and action.

Loving Water across Religions

Contributions to an Integral Water Ethic

Elizabeth McAnally

ORBIS BOOKS
Maryknoll, New York 10545

Founded in 1970, Orbis Books endeavors to publish works that enlighten the mind, nourish the spirit, and challenge the conscience. The publishing arm of the Maryknoll Fathers and Brothers, Orbis seeks to explore the global dimensions of the Christian faith and mission, to invite dialogue with diverse cultures and religious traditions, and to serve the cause of reconciliation and peace. The books published reflect the views of their authors and do not represent the official position of the Maryknoll Society. To learn more about Maryknoll and Orbis Books, please visit our website at www.maryknollsociety.org.

Manufactured in the United States of America
Manuscript editing and typesetting by Joan Weber Laflamme.

Library of Congress Cataloging-in-Publication Data

Names: McAnally, Elizabeth, author.
Title: Loving water across religions : contributions to an integral water ethic / by Elizabeth McAnally.
Description: Maryknoll, NY : Orbis Books, [2018] | Series: Ecology and justice | Includes bibliographical references and index.
Identifiers: LCCN 2018034655 (print) | LCCN 2018041742 (ebook) | ISBN 9781608337705 (e-book) | ISBN 9781626983076 | ISBN 9781626983076—(paperback)
Subjects: LCSH: Water—Religious aspects. | Water—Moral and ethic aspects.
Classification: LCC BL450 (ebook) | LCC BL450 .M43 2018 (print) | DDC 202/.12—dc23
LC record available at https://lccn.loc.gov/2018034655

For my parents and my grandmothers:

Pamela Jane McAnally (Mama)
Charles Lewis McAnally (Daddy)
Minnie Fae Griffin (Grandma)
Myrtle Iva McAnally (Granny)

In memory of my grandfathers:

Wiley Edward Griffin (Granddaddy)
Charles Remmel McAnally (Grandpa)

Contents

Acknowledgments

This book is the confluence of many relations. I first wish to thank my parents, Charles and Pam McAnally, for their overflowing love and support. I give deep thanks to Dr. Elizabeth Allison, Dr. Sean Kelly, and Dr. David L. Haberman for their guidance and encouragement. Dr. Robert McDermott and Dr. Steven Goodman have been crucial in offering their mentorship. Dr. Irene Klaver holds a special role in awakening my sense of wonder for water. I give thanks to Dr. Sam Mickey for his support and collaboration throughout this project. Many thanks are due to the faculty, students, and alumni of the Philosophy, Cosmology, and Consciousness program at the California Institute of Integral Studies. Thanks to all those in Dr. Allison's "critical support group" who gave valuable feedback. Alena Coons has been extremely helpful with her cheerful and insightful editing support. I offer heartfelt thanks to Dr. Mary Evelyn Tucker and Dr. John Grim, whose inspiration, guidance, and generosity have nourished me tremendously. I am forever grateful for my life partner, Aaron Weiss, and his unfailing commitment, love, and support. I offer endless gratitude to all my relations—especially to water, my friend, teacher, and guide. May any merit that arises from this book benefit all beings.

Introduction

The Global Water Crisis and the Need for an Integral Water Ethic

Water is one of the most precious substances on Earth. Water is the creative matrix out of which life on Earth emerges, nourishing all living beings. Water is an elemental link that connects all life. Water is found throughout the bodies of individual organisms, in the great hydrosphere of Earth, and throughout the vast cosmos (for example, ice on comets, oceans on the moons of Saturn and Jupiter, and oceans of water vapor surrounding black holes).[1] A new study published in the journal *Science* reveals that "a significant fraction of the solar system's water predates the Sun" (as much as 30–50 percent of water on Earth and 60–100 percent of water in comets).[2] This means that some of the water we interact with today is more than 4.6 billion years old. Another recent study in *Science* claims that this ancient water arrived on Earth by means of water-rich, carbonaceous chondrite meteorites

---

[1] "Astronomers Find Largest, Oldest Mass of Water in Universe," *Space.com*, July 22, 2011.

[2] L. Ilsedore Cleeves et al., "The Ancient Heritage of Water Ice in the Solar System," *Science* (September 26, 2014): 1592.

during the early formations of the planet.[3] "The water that makes Earth a majestic blue marble was here from the time of our planet's birth."[4]

Humans depend on water for all essential activities (for example, drinking, eating, cooking, bathing, cleaning, growing food, producing artifacts). All living beings on Earth are largely composed of this vital element. For instance, the amount of water in human bodies "comprises from 75 percent of body weight in infants to 55 percent in elderly."[5] As we age, the amount of water in our bodies decreases. Hydration is crucial for life, as water is necessary for metabolism, the growth of cells, reproduction, and "virtually every chemical reaction in our bodies."[6] Going without water for more than a few days results in lethal dehydration. Water sustains life.

Life thrives within a planet that is abundant with water. Approximately 71 percent of Earth's surface is water.[7] This vast amount of water composing Earth's surface has led systems theorists Stephan Harding and Lynn Margulis to call for a renaming of our planetary home as Water Gaia or more simply Water.[8] In a similar vein biogeochemist Vladimir Ivanovich Vernadsky called life "animated water."[9] Water is the

[3] Adam R. Sarafian et al., "Early Accretion of Water in the Inner Solar System from a Carbonaceous Chondrite–like Source," *Science* (October 31, 2014): 623–26.

[4] Andrew Fazekas, "Mystery of Earth's Water Origin Solved," *National Geographic* (October 30, 2014).

[5] Barry M. Popkin, Kristen E. D'Anci, and Irwin H. Rosenberg, "Water, Hydration and Health," *Nutrition Reviews* 68 (8), 2010: 439–58.

[6] Neil Shubin, *The Universe Within: Discovering the Common History of Rocks, Planets, and People* (New York: Pantheon Books, 2013), 41.

[7] US Geological Survey, "How Much Water Is There on, in, and above the Earth?" (December 2, 2016), https://water.usgs.gov/edu/earthhowmuch.html.

[8] Stephan Harding and Lynn Margulis, "Water Gaia: 3.5 Thousand Million Years of Wetness on Planet Earth," in *Gaia in Turmoil: Climate Change, Biodepletion, and Earth Ethics in an Age of Crisis*, ed. Eileen Crist and H. Bruce Rinker (Cambridge, MA: MIT Press, 2010), 57.

[9] Ibid., 43.

source of life and the sustaining element of all living beings. Water is life.

Life actively participates in the hydrological cycle and keeps water on Earth. While life needs water to survive, water needs life to keep it on Earth. As Harding and Margulis argue:

> Life has vigorously helped maintain abundant water on the Earth's surface over the last three and a half thousand million years. . . . Without life's involvement in complex geological, atmospheric, and metabolic processes, Earth would long ago have lost its water, becoming a dry and barren world much like Mars and Venus.[10]

They explain that trees and plants influence the hydrological cycle through processes of evapotranspiration (moving water up from roots through tree trunks and plant stems and releasing vapor through pores on the underside of leaves).[11] Furthermore, organisms help retain water in soil, while certain bacteria like *Pseudomonas syringae* promote the process of rain and snow formation.[12]

Water exists on Earth as a liquid (oceans, lakes, rivers), solid (ice, snow, hail), and gas (clouds, water vapor). All waters are connected through the hydrological cycle, which is "the largest movement of any substance on Earth."[13] While Earth has such a great amount of water covering its surface (71%), almost all of this water is found in the salty oceans. Indeed, 97.5 percent of water on Earth is ocean saltwater; only 2.5 percent of Earth's water is freshwater. The majority of freshwater found on Earth is either solidified in glaciers,

---

[10] Ibid., 41.

[11] Ibid., 44.

[12] Ibid., 45.

[13] Moustafa T. Chahine, "The Hydrological Cycle and Its Influence on Climate," *Nature* 359 (October 1, 1992): 373.

ice caps, and snow (70%) or located underground in aquifers (30%). Only 0.3 percent of freshwater is surface water contained in lakes and rivers (thus available for humans to use in a renewable way); this accounts for only .008 percent of the total water on Earth.[14] Water is renewable yet finite.

THE GLOBAL WATER CRISIS

For the majority of history the very small percentage of Earth's freshwater has been more than enough to provide for the needs of humans and other living beings. However, beginning with the Industrial Revolution in the late eighteenth century, water has become more and more stressed by the growing human population and the rising trend of overconsumption, as well as the ever-increasing rate of urbanization, industrialization, and privatization. These factors contribute to the global water crisis, which includes multiple interrelated crises pertaining to issues of the pollution of freshwater and the oceans, the overpumping of aquifers and the damming and diversion of rivers, the scarcity of freshwater, and the uncertain effects of climate change on the hydrological cycle.[15]

The World Resources Institute warns, "The world's thirst for water is likely to become one of the most pressing resource issues of the twenty-first century."[16] Water experts

---

[14] US Geological Survey "The Water Cycle: Freshwater Storage" (December 2, 2016), https://water.usgs.gov/edu/watercyclefreshstorage.html.

[15] For the primary direct and indirect drivers of the water crisis, see Millennium Ecosystem Assessment, *Ecosystems and Human Well-being: Wetlands, and Water Synthesis* (Washington, DC: World Resources Institute, 2005), 6.

[16] Maude Barlow and Tony Clark, *Blue Gold: The Fight to Stop the Corporate Theft of the World's Water* (New York: The New Press, 2002), 15.

Maude Barlow and Tony Clark write, "The global fresh water crisis looms as perhaps the greatest threat ever to the survival of our planet."[17] And as Indian scholar and environmental activist Vandana Shiva notes, "The water crisis is the most pervasive, most severe, and most invisible dimension of the ecological devastation of the earth."[18]

In what follows I share a brief overview of the global water crisis to give a sense of the magnitude and complexity of the crisis. This crisis involves multiple dimensions, including (but not limited to) freshwater scarcity, the need for safe drinking water and sanitation, pollution, and climate change. These dimensions arise from unsustainable ways of using water and in habits of thinking that consider water to be an infinite and inexhaustible resource rather than a fundamental element of life that deserves respect and care. As water expert Jeremy Schmidt explains, "For years water was considered as renewable as sunlight or wind, and the potential for its development seemed limitless. Now, having manipulated water for irrigation, energy, and burgeoning urban centers, we face the reality that although freshwater is renewable, it is as finite as many other resources."[19] Recognizing that the amount of water on Earth is finite demands a shift in values; humans need to learn to regard water not as a resource to be exploited but as a source of life to be cared for. This book points to ways of cultivating a respectful and reverential relationship with water through an ethic rooted in an integral approach to ecology.

---

[17] Ibid., xii.

[18] Vandana Shiva, *Water Wars: Privatization, Pollution, and Profit* (Cambridge, MA: South End Press, 2002), 1.

[19] Jeremy Schmidt, "Water Ethics and Water Management," in *Water Ethics: Foundational Readings for Students and Professionals*, ed. Peter Brown and Jeremy Schmidt (Washington, DC: Island Press, 2010), 3.

ALLOCATING WATER FOR AGRICULTURE, INDUSTRY, AND DOMESTIC USES

When considering freshwater use, it is helpful to note that an estimated 70 percent of water worldwide is withdrawn for agriculture, 22 percent for industry, and 8 percent for domestic uses.[20] The distinction between consumptive and nonconsumptive uses of freshwater is important to clarify. Domestic and some industrial uses of water (for example, thermoelectric cooling) are more nonconsumptive—much of the water used for these purposes returns to the watershed or water system in a usable way. On the other hand, agriculture and the fossil-fuel industry are highly consumptive of water, meaning that water used in these sectors is permanently removed from its local watershed. For example, the water used for agriculture is not reintegrated into the same watershed from which it is retrieved; instead, it is transformed into agricultural products. Agricultural irrigation "is the dominant cause of water depletions and scarcity, accounting for more than 90 percent of all water consumption globally."[21]

Water used for irrigation is often pumped from an aquifer, a subterranean "geological formation containing enough saturated porous and permeable material to transmit water at a rate sufficient to feed a spring or for economic extraction by a well."[22] The phenomenon that occurs when the amount of water withdrawn from an aquifer exceeds the amount of that aquifer's recharge is called *overdrafting,* and it causes several problems: arsenic, fluoride, and radon are found in water that is drawn from lower levels in the aquifer; salt water can

---

[20] Christiana Zenner, *Just Water: Theology, Ethics, and Fresh Water Crises* (Maryknoll, NY: Orbis Books, 2018), 33.

[21] Brian D. Richter et al., "Tapped Out: How Can Cities Secure Their Water Future?" *Water Policy* 15 (2013): 337.

[22] Robert Glennon, *Water Follies: Groundwater Pumping and the Fate of America's Fresh Waters* (Washington, DC: Island Press, 2002), 237.

infiltrate water tables along coastal regions; and land subsidence (the cracking or dropping of the land surface) often occurs as the water table diminishes.[23] Thus, overdrafting is an unsustainable practice that contributes to freshwater scarcity.

FRESHWATER SCARCITY, SAFE DRINKING WATER, AND SANITATION

The scarcity of freshwater to meet the vital needs of humans and the Earth community is an existential threat. UN-Water notes, "Water use has been growing at more than twice the rate of population increase in the last century," and by 2025, water scarcity will affect 1.8 billion people.[24] A major cause of water scarcity is pollution from urban, industrial, and agricultural sources.[25] In addition to pollution, the scarcity of freshwater "often has its roots in water shortage, and it is in the arid and semi-arid regions affected by droughts and wide climate variability, combined with population growth and economic development, that the problems of water scarcity are most acute."[26] Water scarcity is most prevalent in the Near East, North Africa, South Africa, Mexico, Pakistan, India, and China.[27]

The United Nations reports that in 2015, 800 million people did not have access to an improved water source, and 2.5 billion people on the planet lived without improved sanitation.[28] An "improved drinking water source" is one that

---

[23] Ibid., 32–33, 241.

[24] UN-Water, "Coping with Water Scarcity: A Strategic Issue and Priority for System-wide Action" (August 2006), 2.

[25] Ibid.

[26] Ibid.

[27] Ibid.

[28] Reza Ardakanian, Jens Liebe, and Lis Mullin Bernhardt, eds., "Report on the Achievements during the International Decade for Action: Water for Life 2005–2015," UN-Water (March 2015), 19.

"adequately protects the source from outside contamination, particularly faecal matter."[29] Examples of improved drinking water sources include water piped into one's home or plot, public tap, tubewell or borehole, protected dug well, protected spring, and rainwater collection. On the other hand, the drinking water source is unimproved if it is an unprotected dug well or spring, surface water, tanker truck, or bottled water.[30]

The majority of people who do not have access to improved drinking water are rural dwellers (653 million people).[31] Of those without access to improved drinking water, 40 percent live in sub-Saharan Africa.[32] Women and girls are primarily responsible for collecting water when an improved drinking water source is not available (71 percent of cases).[33] The average roundtrip time to collect water is thirty minutes, and often several trips each day are required.[34] This demands time and energy that could be devoted to other activities such as education, household tasks, earning wages, and recreation. Also, water is significantly heavy (1 liter of water weighs 1 kilogram; 1 gallon weighs 8.36 pounds), and because water is often carried in containers on the head, this task leads to neck and back pain, musculoskeletal disorders, and physical injuries.[35]

---

[29] UNICEF and World Health Organization, "Progress on Drinking Water and Sanitation: 2012 Update" (2012), 33.

[30] Ibid.

[31] Ibid., 12.

[32] Ibid., 61.

[33] Ibid., 36.

[34] Ibid.

[35] Jo-Anne L. Geere, Paul R. Hunter, and Paul Jagals, "Domestic Water Carrying and Its Implications for Health: A Review and Mixed Methods Pilot Study in Limpopo Province, South Africa," *Environmental Health* 9 (2010): 52.

An improved sanitation facility "hygienically separates human excreta from human contact."[36] Examples of improved sanitation include the use of flush or pour-flush to a piped sewer system, septic tank, or pit latrine (as opposed to flushing elsewhere); ventilated improved pit latrine; pit latrine with a slab (as opposed to without a slab); and composting toilet. Unimproved sanitation includes open defecation (that is, having no sanitation facility), bucket, hanging toilet or latrine, and shared or public facilities.[37] The majority of those without improved sanitation are rural inhabitants (1.8 billion people) of sub-Saharan Africa, Southern Asia, and Eastern Asia.[38]

Those who rely upon an unclean source of drinking water or do not have improved sanitation facilities are subject to debilitating and sometimes fatal waterborne diseases, including diarrhea, cholera, schistosomiasis, *E. coli* infection, and dysentery. The World Health Organization (WHO) reports, "Diarrhoeal disease is the second leading cause of death in children under five years old," killing an estimated 760,000 young children each year. WHO goes on to say, "A significant proportion of diarrhoeal disease can be prevented through safe drinking-water and adequate sanitation and hygiene."[39] In light of the deleterious effects of living without proper sanitation, it is quite disturbing to note the results of a United Nations study in 2013 that more people have cell phones than toilets. "Of the world's seven billion people, six billion have mobile phones," while 2.5 billion do not have access to toilets; and of

---

[36] UNICEF and World Health Organization, "Progress on Drinking Water and Sanitation," 33.

[37] Ibid.

[38] Centers for Disease Control and Prevention, "Global WASH Fast Facts"; UNICEF and World Health Organization, "Progress on Drinking Water and Sanitation," 23.

[39] World Health Organization, "Diarrhoeal Disease" (April 2013).

those without sanitation, "1.1 billion people still defecate in the open."[40] Of those practicing open defecation, 949 million live in rural areas, 60 percent of whom live in India.[41]

The lack of improved sanitation has social justice consequences. Because there is a lack of improved sanitation facilities in India, women who work in urban areas must wait to urinate until they get home after a full day's work, thus increasing the possibility of bladder and urinary-tract infections.[42] Furthermore, "the number one reason that girls drop out of school is because there are no toilets."[43] Also, the lack of toilet facilities is directly connected to public safety. Women who need to urinate at night must go out into the fields to do so, and this makes them vulnerable to the dangers of rape and assault.[44]

As the United Nations Children's Fund (UNICEF) and WHO note, the following efforts are needed to address the urgent need for improved drinking water and sanitation: "[to] reduce urban-rural disparities and inequities associated with poverty; to dramatically increase coverage in countries in sub-Saharan Africa and Oceania; to promote global monitoring of drinking water quality; to bring sanitation 'on track'; and to look beyond the MDG [Millennium Development Goal] target towards universal coverage."[45] These efforts are crucial for human health and well-being. As Vandana Shiva

---

[40] United Nations News Centre, "Deputy UN Chief Calls for Urgent Action to Tackle Global Sanitation Crisis" (March 21, 2013).

[41] UNICEF and World Health Organization, "Progress on Drinking Water and Sanitation," 19–20.

[42] Chhavi Sachdev, "Women in India Agitate for Their Right to Pee," PRI's *The World* (November 25, 2014).

[43] Ibid.

[44] Eleanor Goldberg, "Toilets Could Protect Women in India from Getting Raped," The Huffington Post (September 3, 2014).

[45] UNICEF and World Health Organization, "Progress on Drinking Water and Sanitation," 2.

explains, "For Third World women, water scarcity means traveling longer distances in search of water. For peasants, it means starvation and destitution as drought wipes out their crops. For children, it means dehydration and death. There is simply no substitute for this precious liquid, necessary for the biological survival of animals and plants."[46]

Water is life, and the lack of clean water and sanitation leads to sickness and death. In light of this reality, in 2010 the United Nations General Assembly passed a resolution to officially recognize "the right to safe and clean drinking water and sanitation as a human right that is essential for the full enjoyment of life and all human rights."[47] In recognizing this basic human right the United Nations called upon the financial funding and cooperation of states and international organizations to "provide safe, clean, accessible and affordable drinking water and sanitation for all."[48]

POLLUTION

The pollution of waterways is a major factor in the global water crisis. There are two main types of water pollution: point source pollution and nonpoint source pollution. Point source pollution is a specific, identifiable source of pollution (e.g., an oil spill in the ocean or sewage discharged from factories). Nonpoint source pollution, on the other hand, is diffuse and difficult to identify, occurring when rain or snowmelt flows over the ground and "picks up and carries away natural and human-made pollutants, finally depositing them into lakes, rivers, wetlands, coastal waters and ground

---

[46] Shiva, *Water Wars*, 15.

[47] United Nations General Assembly, "Resolution Adopted by the General Assembly on 28 July 2010: '64/292. The Human Right to Water and Sanitation'" (August 3, 2010), 2.

[48] Ibid., 3.

waters."[49] Examples of nonpoint source pollution include the chemical runoff from fertilizers, herbicides, and insecticides from agricultural fields, as well as grease and oil runoff from parking lots.

The major pollutants in water are "nutrients, pathogens, heavy metals, organic pollutants and micro-pollutants found in wastes and wastewater from humans and economic activities such as agriculture, industry, mining, and other sectors such as pharmacy. Indeed untreated wastewater is one of the biggest sources of water pollution."[50] It is a grim fact that in the twenty-first century, "90 percent of wastewater produced in the Third World is still discharged, untreated, into local rivers and streams."[51] The main causes of pollution are "population growth, increased economic activity, intensification and expansion of agriculture, and increased sewerage connections with no or low levels of treatment."[52] The health risks from drinking and coming into contact with polluted water are severe. Those who are most vulnerable to the impacts of water pollution are women, children, and low-income rural people, especially fishers.[53]

Pollution is rampant with industrialized agriculture, which promotes the widespread use of fertilizers that are high in nitrates. When fertilizers run off agricultural fields and drain into waterways, they lead to algae overgrowths. These algae blooms consume large amounts of oxygen in the water, creating dead zones (hypoxic, or low oxygen, zones) in which a majority of marine life cannot exist. This is particularly

---

[49] US Environmental Protection Agency, "Basic Information about Nonpoint Source (NPS) Pollution," August 10, 2018, https://www.epa.gov.

[50] UN-Water, "Towards a Worldwide Assessment of Freshwater Quality: A UN-Water Analytical Brief," 2016, 6.

[51] Barlow and Clark, *Blue Gold*, 30.

[52] UN-Water, "Towards a Worldwide Assessment of Freshwater Quality," 8.

[53] Ibid.

evident in the case of the Mississippi River Delta at the Gulf of Mexico. The Mississippi River watershed drains the water of roughly 40 percent of the continental United States.[54] Much of the land within this watershed is farmland, and the widespread use of industrial fertilizers on these farms leads to the draining of chemicals into the river, concentrating heavily in the delta. As a result, the Gulf of Mexico currently has the second largest dead zone in the world.[55] The Baltic Sea has the largest dead zone in the world, "where nutrient-enriched runoff from farms has combined with nitrogen deposition from the burning of fossil fuels and human waste discharged directly into the sea's waters."[56] Pollution from fertilizers is common to many waterways throughout the world. *National Geographic* reports this dire statistic:

> One billion pounds (about half a billion kilograms) of industrial weed and bug killers are used throughout the United States every year, and most of it runs off into the country's water systems. Because of pollutants like this, nearly 40% of U.S. rivers and streams are too dangerous for fishing, swimming, or drinking, and fish and other water-dwelling wildlife have become living toxic-waste carriers.[57]

Oceans around the world are also heavily polluted with trash. Some of this pollution is illegally dumped or accidentally spills into the ocean from ships or offshore oil rigs. Furthermore, "virtually every kind of plastic packaging and plastic

---

[54] Christopher J. Woltemade, "Mississippi River Basin," http://www.waterencyclopedia.com.

[55] Brian Clark Howard, "Mississippi Basin Water Quality Declining Despite Conservation," *National Geographic* (April 12, 2014).

[56] Cheryl Lyn Dybas, "Dead Zones Spreading in World Oceans," *BioScience* 55, no. 7 (2005): 554.

[57] Barlow and Clark, *Blue Gold*, 29.

object used on land may be discarded or lost to the sea."[58] Among the five major ocean gyres where currents converge, the North Pacific Gyre holds within it the Great Pacific Garbage Patch (also called the Pacific trash vortex), which "spans waters from the West Coast of North America to Japan. The patch is actually comprised of the Western Garbage Patch, located near Japan, and the Eastern Garbage Patch, located between the U.S. states of Hawaii and California."[59] This "soup" of garbage is composed of a vast variety of debris, including fishing nets, single-use plastic bags, toothbrushes, shoes, boat scraps, and nurdles (preproduction microplastic resin pellets). Approximately 80 percent of the pollution in the Great Pacific Garbage Patch comes from activities on land in North America and Asia.[60]

The main component of marine debris is plastic, for two main reasons: "First, plastic's durability, low cost, and malleability mean that it's being used in more and more consumer and industrial products. Second, plastic goods do not biodegrade but instead break down into smaller pieces."[61] Once plastic is created, it cannot be destroyed naturally but instead breaks down into smaller and smaller particles. Insects, fish, birds, and sea turtles may then eat pieces of plastic, mistaking them for food, which can lead to fatal choking or starvation.[62] The bioaccumulation of plastics within the food chain is

---

[58] Robert H. Day, David G. Shaw, and Steven E. Ignell, "The Quantitative Distribution and Characteristics of Neustonic Plastic in the North Pacific Ocean, 1985–88," *Proceedings of the Second International Conference on Marine Debris,* 2–7 April 1989, Honolulu, Hawaii, ed. Richard S. Shomura and Mary Lynne Godfrey (National Oceanic and Atmospheric Administration, 1990), 1:248.

[59] "Great Pacific Garbage Patch," *National Geographic* (n.d.), nationalgeographic.com.

[60] Ibid.

[61] Ibid.

[62] Day, Shaw, and Ignell, "Quantitative Distribution and Characteristics of Neustonic Plastic in the North Pacific Ocean, 1985–88," 262–63.

extremely problematic, for when small animals ingest plastic and then larger animals prey on multiple smaller animals that have eaten plastic, the amount of toxic material concentrates within the larger animal. This bioaccumulation continues up the food chain, harming aquatic animals and humans alike. The 2018 film *Albatross* documents the effects of this ocean pollution on the albatrosses of Midway Island in the Pacific Ocean, noting how droves of these birds are dying from eating plastics. The filmmakers create a vivid image of the harmful effects of plastic pollution by dissecting the corpses of many of these birds to show bellies full of plastic trash. In working toward the well-being of the Earth community, water pollution must be addressed and remedied.

CLIMATE CHANGE

Climate change is very much a water issue. As the chair of UN-Water, Zafar Adeel, explains, "Climate change is all about water, and we have to make that connection."[63] Global climate change has numerous uncertain effects on the hydrological cycle. Erratic weather is more prevalent, bringing unpredictable floods in some regions and severe droughts in others. Many of the fundamental indictors of climate change are water based. For example, as more greenhouse gases are released into the atmosphere, the temperature of the air and ocean rises, which causes glaciers, snow, and ice to melt and sea levels to rise.[64] As the Intergovernmental Panel on Climate Change reports, "The rate of sea level rise since the mid-19th

---

[63] Circle of Blue, "Zafar Adeel: A Conversation with the New Chair of UN-Water" (March 25, 2010).

[64] Intergovernmental Panel on Climate Change, *Climate Change 2014: Synthesis Report. Contribution of Working Groups I, II and III to the Fifth Assessment Report of the Intergovernmental Panel on Climate Change*, Core Writing Team: Rajendra K. Pachauri and Leo Meyer (Geneva: Intergovernmental Panel on Climate Change, 2015).

century has been larger than the mean rate during the previous two millennia."[65] Furthermore, "surface temperature is projected to rise over the 21st century under all assessed emission scenarios. It is very likely that heat waves will occur more often and last longer, and that extreme precipitation events will become more intense and frequent in many regions. The ocean will continue to warm and acidify, and global mean sea level to rise."[66]

The oceans, which have absorbed about half of anthropogenic carbon dioxide emitted since the Industrial Revolution, are becoming more acidic and thus endangering the lives of marine organisms like coral reefs.[67] Ocean acidification is "a process of increasing seawater acidity caused by the uptake of anthropogenic carbon dioxide (CO_2) by the ocean" and "is expected to change surface ocean pH to levels unprecedented for millions of years, affecting marine food web structures and trophic interactions."[68]

Global climate change will affect the poorest peoples of the world the most.[69] As droughts become more common, the women of the developing world will be forced to travel greater distances to find reliable sources of potable water. Many around the world who live in island and coastal communities will be displaced by rising sea levels and will become climate refugees.[70] While the exact number of those who will be affected by the rising seas is not known, it is helpful to

---

[65] Ibid., 2.

[66] Ibid., 10.

[67] "Ocean Acidification: Carbon Dioxide Is Putting Shelled Animals at Risk," *National Geographic* (April 27, 2007).

[68] J. Rafael Bermúdez et al., "Ocean Acidification Reduces Transfer of Essential Biomolecules in a Natural Plankton Community," *Scientific Reports* 6 (27749) (2016): 1.

[69] Shiva, *Water Wars*, 49.

[70] Frank Biermann and Ingrid Boas, "Preparing for a Warmer World: Towards a Global Governance System to Protect Climate Refugees," *Global Environmental Politics* 10, no. 1 (2010): 60–88.

note that the communities of Small Island Developing States (SIDS) compose 5 percent of the global human population, and roughly 44 percent of the global population lives within 150 kilometers (ninety-three miles) of the ocean.[71] As John Tibbetts reports, fourteen of the world's seventeen megacities (cities exceeding ten million people) are in coastal areas, and "two-fifths of the world's major cities of 1–10 million people are also located near coastlines."[72] As the climate continues to change in light of anthropogenic carbon dioxide emissions, the effects on the water cycle will become more apparent, and it will be imperative to respond to the suffering connected to climate change.

OVERVIEW OF BOOK

In light of the global water crisis it is no surprise that tensions concerning access to water are mounting. It has been argued that future wars will be fought not over fossil fuels but over water—"blue gold."[73] In August 1995, Ismail Serageldin, who was at that time the vice president of the World Bank and the chairman of the World Water Commission, made this grim prediction: "We already have 40 percent of the world's population living on rivers shared by more than one country. . . . Many of the wars in this century were about oil, but wars of the next century will be over water."[74]

---

[71] Alliance of Small Island States (AOSIS), "About AOSIS"; "UN Atlas: 44 Percent of Us Live in Coastal Areas" (January 31, 2010).

[72] John Tibbetts, "Coastal Cities: Living on the Edge," *Environmental Health Perspectives* 110, no. 11 (2002): 674.

[73] See Barlow and Clark, *Blue Gold.* For more about the looming threat of water wars, see Brahma Chellaney, *Water, Peace, and War: Confronting the Global Water Crisis,* updated ed. (Lanham, MD: Rowman and Littlefield Publishers, 2015); and Diane Raines Ward, *Water Wars: Drought, Flood, Folly, and the Politics of Thirst* (New York: Riverhead Books, 2002).

[74] Barbara Crossette, "Severe Water Crisis Ahead for Poorest Nations in Next 2 Decades," *New York Times*, August 10, 1995.

As the examples above illustrate, people living in the twenty-first century find themselves in the midst of a global water crisis. "There is simply no way to overstate the fresh water crisis on the planet today," Barlow and Clark argue. "The alarm is sounding. Will we hear it in time?"[75] Given the urgency of the global water crisis, it is imperative that humans reinvent their relationship to water. To respond to the suffering that arises when humans, plants, and animals do not have access to the life-giving waters they need to survive, there must be a shift in how humans perceive and relate to water. Humans must stop viewing water as a mere resource, commodity, and sewer to be exploited and from which to gain profit, and a depository within which to dispose of waste. Offering an alternative to this dominating attitude, this book argues for the need to perceive water as a precious source of life that deserves respect and care. Water's value cannot be measured in terms of economics alone; water also has ecological value, spiritual and religious value, and intrinsic value.

I agree with Aldo Leopold, the American forester, conservationist, and philosopher, when he writes, "It is inconceivable to me that an ethical relation to land can exist without love, respect, and admiration for land, and a high regard for its value."[76] He clarifies that he does not mean "mere economic value" but "value in the philosophical sense."[77] I too argue that water does not have mere economic, instrumental value; water also has "value in the philosophical sense" (intrinsic value).[78] Water is valuable for more than its profitability and usefulness to humans; water is intrinsically valuable in and of itself. An

---

[75] Barlow and Clark, *Blue Gold*, 25.

[76] Aldo Leopold, *A Sand County Almanac and Sketches Here and There* (London: Oxford University Press, 1968), 223.

[77] Ibid.

[78] On the equation of "value in the philosophical sense" and "intrinsic value," see J. Baird Callicott, *Thinking Like a Planet: The Land Ethic and the Earth Ethic* (New York: Oxford University Press, 2013), 37.

ethic based on the wise use of water is an anthropocentric ethic that sees water primarily in terms of instrumental value, asking how humans can use water in a more efficient way. An ethic based on the love of water moves beyond a human-centered approach and has the potential to be Earth-centric and even cosmo-centric, recognizing that all beings have intrinsic value.

Sandra Postel, freshwater expert and founder and director of the Global Water Policy Project, argues that "we need a water ethic" in which we "make the protection of water ecosystems a central goal in all that we do."[79] She goes on to say that "adopting such an ethic would represent a historic philosophical shift away from the strictly utilitarian, divide-and-conquer approach to water management and toward an integrated, holistic approach that views people and water as related parts of a greater whole."[80] In response to Postel's call for an integrated, holistic water ethic, this book is an exploration into such an integral water ethic.

I draw from an integral approach to ecology that studies water and all phenomena from a transdisciplinary perspective and values contributions not only from natural sciences and social sciences, but also from the humanities. Furthermore, an integral approach values multicultural perspectives and multiple ways of knowing. Integral ecologies are "a variety of emerging approaches to ecology that cross disciplinary boundaries in efforts to deeply understand and creatively respond to the complex matters, meanings, and mysteries of relationships that constitute the whole of the Earth community."[81] In other words, an integral approach to

---

[79] Sandra Postel, *Last Oasis: Facing Water Scarcity* (New York: W. W. Norton Company, 1992), 185.

[80] Ibid.

[81] Sam Mickey, Sean Kelly, and Adam Robbert, "Introduction: The History and Future of Integral Ecologies," in *The Variety of Integral Ecologies: Nature, Culture, and Knowledge in the Planetary Era* (Albany: State University of New York Press, 2017), 1.

ecology is a transdisciplinary engagement in understanding the intertwinement of nature and culture and responding in such a way as to create a flourishing future for all members of the Earth community.

Relating to water in an integral mode entails acknowledging that water (and all phenomena) has not only exterior, objective dimensions but also interior, subjective qualities. Thus, an integral water ethic holds that water is not a mere passive object to be exploited for human purposes; instead, this approach recognizes that water is an active and vital member of the Earth community that has intrinsic value. I am deeply inspired by the integral ecological and cosmological work of the cultural historian Thomas Berry, who writes that "the universe is a communion of subjects, not a collection of objects."[82] I also draw from the integral approaches to ecology as articulated by Mary Evelyn Tucker and John Grim, Leonardo Boff, and Ken Wilber. Recognizing that water has intrinsic value, participates as a vital member of a communion of subjects in the Earth community, and inspires personal experiences and cultural worldviews will help lead humans to interact with water with respect and care.

Throughout, I highlight the contributions of religious traditions to an integral water ethic, noting the importance of myths, rituals, and contemplative practices for cultivating a respectful relationship with water. As I see it, the subjective perspectives offered within religious traditions help humans gain insight into the interior dimension of water. I explore some of the cultural perceptions of water embedded within religions and show how water flows through myths and rituals of initiation and purification. Furthermore, I consider how an integral water ethic can be cultivated through contemplative

---

[82] Thomas Berry, *Evening Thoughts: Reflecting on Earth as Sacred Community*, ed. Mary Evelyn Tucker (San Francisco: Sierra Club Books and University of California Press, 2006), 17.

practices that enable one to have a deeper sense of intimacy and empathy with water and the Earth community.

I argue that an integral water ethic involves an attitude that brings water into one's awareness and concern and is crucial to the development of mutually enhancing relations between humans and water. This is a way to enter into the interior dimension of water itself. Throughout this book, I give special attention to personal experiences, cultural attitudes, religious myths and rituals, and ethical impulses that inform relationships with water. By exploring these subjective dimensions of reality, I argue that they can and should play crucial roles in discourses surrounding water. Personal experiences and cultural worldviews are needed (just as much as objective perspectives from economics, politics, ecology, biology, and other disciplines) when working to determine appropriate actions toward particular bodies of water. Listening to and representing the many voices of water is necessary for addressing water issues in creative, effective, and democratic ways. The purpose of my investigation is to explore creative avenues for cultivating mutually enhancing relations between humans and water and thereby to help overcome our current destructive attitude toward the natural world.

In Chapter 1, I contextualize an integral water ethic within an integral approach to ecology. I also give an account of the methodological approach and significance of this book. In the following three chapters I explore various contributions to an integral water ethic offered by three world religions: Christianity, Hinduism, and Buddhism. In Chapter 2, I focus on the Christian ritual of baptism. I explain how the notion of sacramental consciousness is a helpful entry into an integral water ethic. Chapter 3 focuses on a particular river, the Yamuna River of northern India. I explore cultural attitudes toward the river, the physical state of the river, and Hindu religious responses to the pollution of the river. I highlight the value of *seva* (loving service) for an integral water ethic. Then, in Chapter 4, I explore an integral water ethic in connection with the Buddhist archetype of the bodhisattva who acts wisely and compassionately for the benefit of all beings. I argue that we need wisdom and compassion for all beings, including water, and that water itself can be seen as a wise, compassionate bodhisattva. My approach to an integral water ethic respects the specificity of religious traditions and holds that we can draw from the unique insights of particular religious traditions to find beneficial ways to relate to water.

After considering the contributions of these religious traditions for an integral water ethic, I offer some contemplative practices in Chapter 5 that focus on cultivating a more intimate, loving, and compassionate relationship with water. Finally, in the Conclusion, I summarize my findings and point to possibilities for future research. Throughout this work I describe how an integral water ethic encourages humans to learn to cultivate love and compassion for water and for those suffering from the global water crisis. Through the cultivation of love and compassion for water, humans are better able to see water not as a mere resource and commodity, but rather as a loving and compassionate member of the Earth community that nourishes all beings.

This book is not an attempt to be an exhaustive or definitive account of integral water ethics. Instead, it merely explores one avenue into an integral water ethic. I hope to inspire others to develop further approaches to an integral water ethic.

1

An Integral Ecological Approach to Water

Current discourse about ecological issues in general and water in particular is focused primarily on objective perspectives (economics, policy, science, and so on). While these perspectives are necessary to conversations about responding to water issues, they are not sufficient by themselves. Discourse about water must also include and value subjective perspectives (perspectives from cultural and religious traditions, as well as personal experiences) so that complex water issues can be addressed in holistic ways. Thus, an integral approach to water is needed. As the integral ecologists Sean Esbjörn-Hargens and Michael Zimmerman explain, "Until now, ecologists and ecological discourse have mostly excluded an explicit recognition of interiors and their development—and make no mistake, there is a need to understand our interior individual and collective relationship to the natural world, for it is within our interiors that motivation to treat the natural world in healthier ways resides."[1]

---

[1] Sean Esbjörn-Hargens and Michael E. Zimmerman, *Integral Ecology: Uniting Multiple Perspectives on the Natural World* (Boston, MA: Integral Books, 2009), 7.

By valuing the subjective dimensions of the human being—personal experience and culture—we find resources within ourselves to interact ethically with water and the world. Furthermore, by investigating and valuing our own subjectivity, we can come to realize the subjectivity inherent within water. Our human interiority helps us recognize the interiority and intrinsic value of water.

This chapter situates an integral approach to water within two overlapping fields: (1) integral ecologies and (2) religion and ecology. It is worth noting that there is a plurality of integral approaches to ecology—in other words, *integral ecological diversity*—for no single approach is sufficient for responding to the complex relationships of the Earth community.[2] By studying water in an integral way, humans can learn to better listen and respond to the voices of water and the different perspectives required for cultivating a respectful relationship to water. In this chapter I also provide an account of the methodological approaches that I use throughout this book, and I give an overview of the book's academic, personal, social, and spiritual significance.

I attempt to articulate an integral water ethic by drawing from various perspectives from the world's religions, as well as from relevant contemplative practices. An integral water ethic is needed to complement solely objective perspectives on water gathered from science, policy, and economics. This work is on the path toward an integral approach to water studies, by which I mean an approach that includes transdisciplinary dialogue about water, multicultural perspectives pertaining to water, and multiple ways of knowing water.

---

[2] Sam Mickey, Sean Kelly, and Adam Robbert, "Introduction: The History and Future of Integral Ecologies," in *The Variety of Integral Ecologies: Nature, Culture, and Knowledge in the Planetary Era* (Albany: State University of New York Press, 2017), 20.

Ethical and religious responses to water issues are often left out of the conversation when developing water policy and water management strategies. For example, Integrated Water Resource Management (IWRM) is one of the leading strategies for managing water. This is a globally recognized approach for water management that employs policy, environmental sciences, and social sciences to manage water. The Global Water Partnership's Technical Advisory Committee provides this definition of IWRM: "a process which promotes the co-ordinated development and management of water, land and related resources, in order to maximize the resultant economic and social welfare in an equitable manner without compromising the sustainability of vital ecosystems."[3] IWRM is oriented by objective perspectives while explicitly attempting to exclude noneconomic values and other subjective dimensions.[4] In contrast to this approach, this book focuses on subjective and intersubjective perspectives to water issues (namely, perspectives from personal experiences and religious worldviews) to show how personal and cultural points of view are crucial in developing mutually enhancing relations between humans and water. These subjective perspectives need to be brought into the conversation with objective perspectives such as IWRM in order to find integral ways of relating to water issues.

The global water crisis is a complex phenomenon that includes a number of overlapping aspects (for example, freshwater scarcity, pollution, climate change, and the need for safe drinking water and improved sanitation). In light of the complexity and urgency of the global water crisis, it is imperative that the study of water is undertaken through an

---

[3] Jeremy Schmidt, "Water Ethics and Water Management," in *Water Ethics: Foundational Readings for Students and Professionals*, ed. Peter Brown and Jeremy Schmidt (Washington, DC: Island Press, 2010), 7.

[4] Ibid.

integral lens, including knowledge from as many different perspectives as possible. In this book I explore elements of an integral water ethic through a survey of personal and cultural perspectives on water. In what follows I briefly give an overview of the overlapping fields of integral ecologies and religion and ecology, as well as their tools for studying water.

INTEGRAL ECOLOGIES

In *On the Verge of a Planetary Civilization* philosopher and integral ecologist Sam Mickey gives an account of the history of the phrase *integral ecology*.[5] Mickey notes that in 1995, three publications—by Thomas Berry, Leonardo Boff and Virgilio Elizondo, and Ken Wilber—independently began using the phrase to signify the integration of natural and cultural dimensions of ecology. In what follows I briefly explain these different yet overlapping uses of the phrase.

Thomas Berry, the cultural historian and self-proclaimed "geologian" (Earth scholar), uses the phrases "integral ecology" and "integral cosmology" in describing the place of the human in cosmic evolution.[6] In describing Berry's "integral corpus," Sean Esbjörn-Hargens notes that "phrases like 'integral vision,' 'integral ecological community,' 'integral functioning,' and viewing humans as 'integral members' of the Earth are found throughout his work."[7] Berry explains

---

[5] Sam Mickey, *On the Verge of a Planetary Civilization: A Philosophy of Integral Ecology* (London: Rowman and Littlefield International, 2014), 16–24.

[6] Drew Dellinger, the eco-justice poet, recounts that in 1995 Thomas Berry began "referring to his cosmological vision as an 'integral cosmology or integral ecology.'" In Sean Esbjörn-Hargens, "Ecological Interiority: Thomas Berry's Integral Ecology Legacy," in *Thomas Berry, Dreamer of the Earth: The Spiritual Ecology of the Father of Environmentalism*, ed. Ervin Laszlo and Allan Combs (Rochester, VT: Inner Traditions, 2011), 93.

[7] Ibid., 94.

that the "Great Work" of humans at this present time in history is to become mutually enhancing members of the Earth community. He writes, "The Great Work now, as we move into a new millennium, is to carry out the transition from a period of human devastation of the Earth to a period when humans would be present to the planet in a mutually beneficial manner."[8] Berry goes on to say: "We are not here to control. We are here to become integral with the larger Earth Community."[9]

Berry calls for an "integral Earth study," by which he means a study that can integrate understandings of the "landsphere, the watersphere, the airsphere, the lifesphere, and the mindsphere."[10] While the physical and biological sciences have long studied the first four of these spheres, he argues that the study of Earth is not holistic or integral unless it also includes the sphere of the human mind. Berry elaborates on the roles and actions of the integral ecologist, saying, "We need an ecological spirituality with an integral ecologist as spiritual guide."[11] He goes on to say that the "great spiritual mission of the present is to renew all the traditional religious-spiritual traditions in the context of the integral functioning of the biosystems of the planet."[12] With the aid of the integral ecologist and an integral Earth study, humans can better find an intimate place within the Earth community. Learning to cultivate mutually enhancing relationships with Earth and its inhabitants is core to an integral water ethic wherein humans aspire to interact with water with greater respect and care.

---

[8] Thomas Berry, *The Great Work: Our Way into the Future* (New York: Random House, 1999), 3.

[9] Ibid., 48.

[10] Ibid., 90.

[11] Thomas Berry, *The Sacred Universe: Earth, Spirituality, and Religion in the Twenty-First Century*, ed. Mary Evelyn Tucker (New York: Columbia University Press, 2009), 135.

[12] Ibid., 136.

Berry's integral vision is founded on the cosmogenetic principle that he articulates with the mathematical cosmologist Brian Swimme in *The Universe Story*:

> The cosmogenetic principle states that the evolution of the universe will be characterized by *differentiation, autopoiesis,* and *communion* throughout time and space and at every level of reality. . . . Some synonyms for differentiation are diversity, complexity, variation, disparity, multiform nature, heterogeneity, articulation. Different words that point to the second feature are autopoiesis, subjectivity, self-manifestation, sentience, self-organization, dynamic centers of experience, presence, identity, inner principle of being, voice, interiority. And for the third feature, communion, interrelatedness, interdependence, kinship, mutuality, internal relatedness, reciprocity, complementarity, interconnectivity, and affiliation all point to the same dynamic of cosmic evolution.[13]

The cosmogenetic principle can be explained as follows. As the universe evolves, matter becomes more differentiated. A vast variety of complex manifestations of beings occurs, and with this ongoing differentiation comes increased subjectivity or interiority. "From the shaping of the hydrogen atom to the formation of the human brain, interior psychic unity has consistently increased along with a greater complexification of being."[14] The acts of differentiation and subjectivity that are fundamental to the universe are intertwined with the act of

---

[13] Brian Swimme and Thomas Berry, *The Universe Story: From the Primordial Flaring Forth to the Ecozoic Era—A Celebration of the Unfolding of the Cosmos* (San Francisco: HarperCollins, 1992), 71–72.

[14] Thomas Berry, *The Dream of the Earth* (San Francisco: Sierra Club Books, 1990), 45.

communion, which is seen with the complex interrelatedness of all beings in the universe. There is a "comprehensive unity" of the cosmos: "we live in a *universe—a single, if multiform, energy event.*"[15]

In light of the cosmogenetic principle, Berry summarizes the Great Work of our time: "The future can exist only when we understand the universe as composed of subjects to be communed with, not as objects to be exploited."[16] This idea that we live in a community of subjects is central to Berry's work and to his articulation of integral ecology. It is also a fundamental point of an integral water ethic. As I argue throughout this book, water must not be treated as a mere object that is exploited for profit; instead, the intrinsic value of water must be recognized so that humans can live in communion with this sacred source of life and the cosmos as a whole.

One can see the three aspects of the cosmogenetic principle illuminated in water. Water is a unique element whose chemical and physical structure differentiates it from other substances within the universe. The self-organizing dynamics of water evident in particular patterns like whirlpools, eddies, snowflakes, and waves suggest that water has an interior or subjective dimension. Furthermore, water is in interdependent relationships with other beings throughout the Earth community. The first and third characteristics of cosmogenesis are perhaps the more readily understandable when considering the example of water, but more needs to be said about the interiority of water. To do this, I draw on a passage from the French paleontologist and Jesuit priest Pierre Teilhard de Chardin. With his phenomenological accounts of the universe, Teilhard explains how the material universe is

---

[15] Ibid., 45–46.
[16] Berry, *The Great Work*, x–xi.

permeated with spirit (how subjectivity is inherent within the natural world):

> Indisputably, deep within ourselves, through a rent or tear, an "interior" appears at the heart of beings. This is enough to establish the existence of this interior in some degree or other everywhere forever in nature. Since the stuff of the universe has an internal face at one point in itself, its structure is necessarily *bifacial*; that is, in every region of time and space, as well, for example, as being granular, *coextensive with its outside, everything has an inside.*[17]

Here Teilhard reasons that because humans experience interiority within themselves, this means that interiority is a phenomenon inherent within the cosmos. All things must have some degree of interiority, just as all things have some degree of exteriority. Like every other being in the universe, water has some degree of interiority, an inner state that is predicated on the fact that an external dimension exists. In brief, the cosmogenetic principle concludes that water (and all beings in the cosmos) has exteriority or objective dimensions, interiority or subjective dimensions, and relationality or communion with other beings.

Another related approach to integral ecology is found within the work of the Brazilian liberation theologian Leonardo Boff. In the editorial to a 1995 issue on ecology and poverty in *Concilium: International Journal of Theology*, Boff and his co-author Virgilio Elizondo describe their vision of integral ecology. "The quest today is increasingly for an *integral ecology*," Boff and Elizondo write, one that can create

---

[17] Pierre Teilhard de Chardin, *The Human Phenomenon*, trans. Sarah Appleton-Weber (Brighton: Sussex Academic Press, 1999), 24.

a new alliance between societies and nature, which will result in the conservation of the patrimony of the earth, socio-cosmic well-being, and the maintenance of conditions that will allow evolution to continue on the course it has now been following for some fifteen thousand million years. . . . For an integral ecology, society and culture also belong to the ecological complex. Ecology is, then, the relationship that all bodies, animate and inanimate, natural and cultural, establish and maintain among themselves and with their surroundings.[18]

Thus, an integral ecology seeks to articulate the intertwinement of natural and cultural phenomena and promotes the well-being of the cosmos and all its inhabitants.

Boff is deeply influenced by Berry and also describes integral ecology in terms of cosmogenesis. In the "integral ecology" section of his website, Boff writes, "Three great phases of emergence happen in cosmogenesis and anthropogenesis: (1) Complexity and differentiation, (2) Self-organization and consciousness, (3) Reconnection and relation of all to all." Boff explains that, from the beginning of the universe, "evolution has been creating more and more different and complex beings," and complexity and differentiation describe the exterior dimension of phenomena. Self-organization and consciousness describe the interior nature of things that increases as complexity increases: "The more complex they are the more they self organize, and the more they show their interior nature and posses [*sic*] more and more levels of consciousness." Reconnection and relation describe the way that individuals within the universe relate to one another. Boff notes, "The more complex and conscious one becomes the

---

[18] Leonardo Boff and Virgilio Elizondo, "Ecology and Poverty: Cry of the Earth, Cry of the Poor," *Concilium: International Journal of Theology* 5 (1995): ix–x.

more one relates and reconnects . . . with all things making it so that the universe really becomes a 'uni-verse,' an organic, dynamic, diverse, tense and harmonic totality, a cosmos and not a chaos." In this way Boff's approach to integral ecology, understood through the principle of cosmogenesis, is very similar to Berry's. All things in the universe have some degree of differentiation, self-organization, and relationship.[19]

A third, yet related, integral approach to ecology has been developed by integral theorist Ken Wilber and elaborated by integral philosophers Sean Esbjörn-Hargens and Michael Zimmerman. This approach is based on Wilber's integral theory and the AQAL (all-quadrant, all-level) framework, a system that describes the world and its inhabitants in terms of four quadrants—subjective ("I"), intersubjective ("We"), objective ("It"), and interobjective ("Its")—and three levels (physical, mental, and spiritual).[20] This systematic approach is helpful for understanding ecology because it integrates a variety of different perspectives, including interior and exterior dimensions, as well as individual and collective dimensions. Esbjörn-Hargens and Zimmerman give the following succinct description: "*Integral Ecology is the study of the subjective and objective aspects of organisms in relationship to their intersubjective and interobjective environments at all levels of depth and complexity.*"[21] They note that an integral approach to ecology "need not be contained within any single framework."[22] On the contrary, they hold that there

---

[19] It is worth noting that Pope Francis is directly influenced by Boff and mentions integral ecology throughout his papal encyclical *Laudato Si': On Care for Our Common Home.* See Chapter 2 herein for more about Pope Francis, *Laudato Si'*, and ecological conversion.

[20] Ken Wilber, *Sex, Ecology, Spirituality: The Spirit of Evolution*, 2nd rev. ed. (Boston: Shambhala, 2000), 127–35. Esbjörn-Hargens and Zimmerman, *Integral Ecology*, 45–74.

[21] Esbjörn-Hargens and Zimmerman, *Integral Ecology*, 168–69.

[22] Ibid., 540.

are "a variety of integral ecologies," and they encourage the proliferation of multiple approaches.[23]

In *Integral Ecology*, Esbjörn-Hargens and Zimmerman write, "There is no such thing as 'one tree.'"[24] We can also say that there is no such thing as "one river," "one lake," or "one ocean." Every waterway, every tree, and every being in the universe is composed of a convergence of multiple perspectives. To develop comprehensive, long-term solutions to water issues, an integral approach is needed that can coordinate these perspectives and facilitate cooperation and dialogue between them.

The unique approaches to integral ecologies provided by Berry, Boff, and Wilber converge in their "call to integrate three aspects of ecological phenomena, differentiation ('It/s'), subjectivity ('I'), and communion ('We')," as argued by philosophers Sam Mickey, Sean Kelly, and Adam Robbert in *The Variety of Integral Ecologies*.[25] In other words, the acknowledgment of the exteriority, interiority, and relationality of all things is at the heart of integral ecology. Furthermore, each of these approaches highlights two main facets of integral ecologies: "(1) opposition to any oversimplification of ecological phenomena, and (2) a transdisciplinary engagement with the sciences, technologies, philosophies, institutions, religions, and personal activities that are woven into the irreducible complexity and multidimensionality of relationships in the natural world."[26] Thus, these approaches to integral ecologies agree on the complex nature of all things and the need to have a transdisciplinary approach to studying ecology.

Integral ecologies demonstrate the importance of including not only objective perspectives but also subjective

---

[23] Ibid., 667.
[24] Ibid., 180.
[25] Mickey, Kelly, and Robbert, "Introduction," 14.
[26] Ibid.

perspectives when studying water. Human interiority and the interiority of water are aspects that I highlight throughout this book, focusing on how the cultivation of respect and care for water can assist in the recognition of the subjectivity of water. By situating this book in the context of an integral approach to ecology, I highlight aspects of personal experiences and religious worldviews that can be foundational to the cultivation of an integral water ethic.

RELIGION AND ECOLOGY

The field of religion and ecology can be seen as one example of an integral approach to ecology. As Mickey, Kelly, and Robbert write in *The Variety of Integral Ecologies,* "Integral approaches to ecology are also emerging in fields of religious studies, specifically in the field of religion and ecology."[27] John Grim and Mary Evelyn Tucker describe this field in *Ecology and Religion*:

> In the last two decades, scholars in religious studies, history of religions, philosophy, and theology are creating a field of religion and ecology with implications for policy and practice. Religion and ecology, as an academic field and as an engaged force, is growing rapidly. . . . The potential of the field and force of world religions and ecology is varied and significant. These studies broaden our understanding of religion, ground cosmological awareness in relation to ecology, offer fresh insight into holism and particularly in nature, and engage environmental issues with an ethical ecological awareness.[28]

---

[27] Ibid., 18.
[28] John Grim and Mary Evelyn Tucker, *Ecology and Religion* (Washington, DC: Island Press, 2014), 10.

The transdisciplinary field of religion and ecology brings the study of religion into dialogue with natural and social sciences. Such an integral approach is needed so that multiple perspectives can collaborate with one another to work together on water issues. A one-sided solution to any problem is rarely sufficient, for a variety of issues may be overlooked in the process.

The environmental crisis, as Tucker explains in *Worldly Wonder,* "calls the religions of the world to respond by finding their voice within the larger Earth community. In so doing, the religions are now entering their ecological phase and finding their planetary expression. They are awakening to a renewed appreciation of matter as a vessel for the sacred."[29] Seeing the physical world as a manifestation or expression of the divine has the potential to lead religions to a more respectful and reverential relationship with the world.

The field of religion and ecology has been growing for the past thirty years. For example, Eugene Hargrove edited *Religion and Environmental Crisis* in 1986.[30] Middlebury College in Vermont hosted a four-day symposium entitled "Spirit and Nature: Religion, Ethics, and Environmental Crisis" in 1990,[31] and a collection of the papers from this symposium was published in 1992 in the edited volume by Steven Rockefeller and John Elder entitled *Spirit and Nature.*[32] The American Academy of Religion (AAR) witnessed the emergence of a Religion and Ecology Consultation in 1991, which developed

---

[29] Mary Evelyn Tucker, *Worldly Wonder: Religions Enter Their Ecological Phase*, Second Master Hsüan Hua Memorial Lecture (Chicago: Open Court, 2003), 9.

[30] Eugene C. Hargrove, ed., *Religion and Environmental Crisis* (Athens: University of Georgia Press, 1986).

[31] Ari L. Goldman, "Religions and Environment: Focus on a Worldly Concern," *The New York Times*, September 17, 1990.

[32] Steven Rockefeller and John Elder, eds., *Spirit and Nature: Why the Environment Is a Religious Issue* (Boston: Beacon Press, 1992).

into the Religion and Ecology Group soon afterward.[33] In 1993, Mary Evelyn Tucker and John Grim edited *Worldviews and Ecology*.[34] In 1996, Roger Gottlieb edited *This Sacred Earth*.[35] And in 2001, Tucker and Grim edited a special issue of the journal *Daedalus* entitled "Religion and Ecology: Can the Climate Change?"[36]

Mary Evelyn Tucker and John Grim, senior scholars at Yale University and students of Thomas Berry, have played a crucial role in the initiation and cultivation of this field of study. Tucker and Grim organized a series of conferences on the intersection of religion and ecology at Harvard University's Center for the Study of World Religions from 1996 through 1998, bringing together over eight hundred scholars and activists and publishing the conference papers in a ten-volume book series.[37] Tucker and Grim make explicit the intention of these conferences and book series in the series foreword of the Harvard volumes:

> The conferences and volumes in the series Religions of the World and Ecology are thus intended to expand the discussion already under way in certain circles and to invite further collaboration on a topic of common concern—the fate of the earth as a religious responsibility. To broaden and deepen the reflective basis for mutual collaboration has been an underlying aim of

---

[33] American Academy of Religion, "Religion and Ecology Group," https://papers.aarweb.org/content/religion-and-ecology-unit.

[34] Mary Evelyn Tucker and John Grim, eds., *Worldviews and Ecology: Religion, Philosophy and the Environment* (Lewisburg, PA: Bucknell University Press, 1993).

[35] Roger S. Gottlieb, ed., *This Sacred Earth: Religion, Nature, Environment* (New York: Routledge, 1996).

[36] Mary Evelyn Tucker and John Grim, eds., "Religion and Ecology: Can the Climate Change?" *Daedalus* 130, no. 4 (2001).

[37] See Forum on Religion and Ecology at Yale, "About Us," http://fore.yale.edu/about-us/.

the conferences themselves. . . . We hope that these conferences and volumes will be simply a beginning of further study of conceptual and symbolic resources, methodological concerns, and practical directions for meeting this environmental crisis.[38]

In 1998, at the conclusion of the conference series, Tucker and Grim founded the Forum on Religion and Ecology. The Forum on Religion and Ecology seeks to bring about dialogue between religions and other perspectives (such as those of the ecological sciences, education, gender studies, and ethics) so that environmental issues can be engaged in comprehensive ways.[39]

The Forum on Religion and Ecology, which began at Harvard University and is now based at Yale University, continues the initial work that was set out at these conferences, acting as a hub to connect scholars and environmentalists from around the world to engage in dialogue concerning the intersection of the world's religious traditions and ecology. The Forum has been responsible for organizing numerous conferences, as well as publishing books, articles, films, newsletters, and a comprehensive website. I have been working directly with this organization since 2006, conducting research, editing the Forum newsletters, and managing the website.

Scholars in the field of religion and ecology have contributed research concerning the role of water in religious traditions. For example, research has been undertaken about the Ganges and the Yamuna rivers in India, rivers that have been traditionally worshiped as sacred. They are now extremely

---

[38] Mary Evelyn Tucker and John Grim, "Series Foreword," in *Buddhism and Ecology: The Interconnection of Dharma and Deeds*, ed. Mary Evelyn Tucker and Duncan Ryûken Williams (Cambridge, MA: Center for the Study of World Religions and Harvard University Press, 1997), xxx–xxxi.

[39] Ibid.

polluted. Kelly Alley provides a case study about the Ganges River in *On the Banks of the Ganga*, and David Haberman offers a case study about the Yamuna River in *River of Love in an Age of Pollution*.[40] In *The Sea Can Wash Away All Evils*, Kimberly C. Patton explores cross-cultural myths about the ocean in light of current marine pollution.[41] Christiana Zenner considers insights about the global water crisis from the Catholic tradition in *Just Water*.[42] In *Deep Blue,* an edited volume by Sylvie Shaw and Andrew Francis, authors discuss the role of water for nature religions.[43]

In *Troubled Waters*, Gary Chamberlain provides a survey of how each of the world's religious traditions relates to water in fundamental ways.[44] For instance, creation stories in religious traditions are often centered on water. In the *Rig Veda*, an ancient text of the Hindu tradition written between 1500 and 1200 BCE, it is said, "Darkness was there, all wrapped around by darkness, and all was Water indiscriminate."[45] The Jewish creation story in the first chapter of the Book of

---

[40] Kelly D. Alley, *On the Banks of the Ganga: When Wastewater Meets a Sacred River* (Ann Arbor: University of Michigan Press, 2002); David L. Haberman, *River of Love in an Age of Pollution: The Yamuna River of Northern India* (Berkeley and Los Angeles: University of California Press, 2006). I discuss Haberman's work at length in Chapter 3 of this book.

[41] Kimberly C. Patton, *The Sea Can Wash Away All Evils: Modern Marine Pollution and the Ancient Cathartic Ocean* (New York: Columbia University Press, 2007).

[42] Christiana Zenner, *Just Water: Theology, Ethics, and Fresh Water Crises* (Maryknoll, NY: Orbis Books, 2018).

[43] Sylvie Shaw and Andrew Francis, eds., *Deep Blue: Critical Reflections on Nature, Religion, and Water* (London: Equinox Publishing, 2008).

[44] Gary L. Chamberlain, *Troubled Waters: Religion, Ethics, and the Global Water Crisis* (Lanham, MD: Rowman and Littlefield Publishers, 2008).

[45] *Rig Veda* X.129, verse 3. This translation is by Raimon Panikkar. See Raimon Panikkar, *Hinduism: Part One: The Vedic Experience: Mantramanjari*, Series: Opera Omnia, vol. 4.1 (Maryknoll, NY: Orbis Books, 2016).

Genesis begins with these words: "In the beginning when God created the heavens and the earth, the earth was a formless void and darkness covered the face of the deep, while a wind from God swept over the face of the waters" (1:1–2). The Qur'an, the sacred scripture of Islam, proclaims, "Allah has created every [living] creature from water. . . . And it is He who has created from water a human being and made him [a relative by] lineage and marriage" (24:45; 25:54, Sahih International). Similarly, for a great number of indigenous traditions throughout the world, "Water is the birthplace or the creation of all things, of peoples and of the Earth itself."[46] For example, Chamberlain writes that the Kogi of Columbia understand that they are "formed in the water." Likewise, the Western Shoshone believe that "all the water that comes from the Mother Earth, that's her blood. It's the Mother Earth's blood." Water for the Dogon of Mali "is 'a divine green seed' impregnating the Earth and so '(bringing) forth twin green beings, half man, half serpent'; the male seed, oil, combines in the womb 'with the moisture of the vaginas in a helix symbolizing the creative vibrations.'"[47]

In addition to its central role in creation stories, water plays a crucial part in rituals of initiation and purification. Historian of religion Mircea Eliade reflects on the purifying power of water when he writes, "In water everything is 'dissolved,' every 'form' is broken up, everything that has happened ceases to exist. . . . Breaking up all forms, doing away with all the past, water possesses this power of purifying, of regenerating, of giving new birth."[48] Various examples of water rituals of purification and initiation include Christian baptism, the

---

[46] Chamberlain, *Troubled Waters*, 13.

[47] Ibid.

[48] Mircea Eliade, *Patterns in Comparative Religion*, trans. Rosemary Sheed (New York: Meridian Books/The World Publishing Company, 1963), 194.

Jewish *mikveh* bath, the Muslim ritual wash of *faraid al-wudu*, sweat lodges of many Native American traditions, and drinking and ritually bathing in the sacred rivers in India.

In my investigations I explore the role of water within religious traditions to see what they can contribute to an integral water ethic. One of the aims of this book is to contribute to the interdisciplinary field of religion and ecology by focusing on the cultivation of an intimate relationship with water and our Earth community.

THEORETICAL PERSPECTIVES AND METHODOLOGICAL APPROACHES

I write from an integral approach to ecology, drawing on the work of Thomas Berry, Leonardo Boff, Ken Wilber, and Mary Evelyn Tucker and John Grim. I use an integral approach to include first-, second-, and third-person perspectives on water. I integrate personal experiences, the perspectives of different religious traditions, and scientific perspectives on water. I approach this book primarily through the following two methodologies: (1) the threefold process of retrieval, reevaluation, and reconstruction within the field of religion and ecology; and (2) organic inquiry. In what follows I briefly explain how these methodologies assist my research.

The threefold process of retrieval, reevaluation, and reconstruction is central to the field of religion and ecology. Mary Evelyn Tucker describes this process:

> Careful methodological reflection is needed in considering how to bring forward in coherent and convincing ways the resources of religious traditions in response to particular aspects of our current environmental crisis. It entails a self-reflexive yet creative approach to retrieving and reclaiming texts and traditions, re-evaluating

and re-examining what will be most efficacious, and thus restoring and reconstructing religious traditions in a creative postmodern world.[49]

In this threefold interpretive method, ecological insights are retrieved from religious traditions. These insights are then reevaluated in terms of whether they are helpful in addressing current environmental issues, and they are reconstructed so as to find novel and creative responses to environmental issues.[50] As Grim and Tucker note, the method of retrieval is descriptive, wherein a researcher highlights concepts and rituals within a religious tradition to draw out the relationship between humans and the natural world.[51] Reevaluation is a prescriptive method that involves assessing the ecologically beneficial and harmful aspects of what has been retrieved (for instance, whether a particular religious tendency is world affirming or world denying).[52] Finally, the prescriptive method of reconstruction entails a creative synthesis or adaptation of religious concepts and practices so that they are more responsive to contemporary environmental issues.[53] I utilize this theoretical methodology in my chapters on Christianity, Hinduism, and Buddhism to interpret religious texts and activism.

I am also approaching this book through the lens of organic inquiry, a qualitative methodology, originally called organic research, developed by Jennifer Clements, Dorothy Ettling, Dianne Jenett, Lisa Shields, and Nora Taylor in 1994.[54] Some of the key features of this method include treating research as

---

[49] Tucker, *Worldly Wonder*, 26.

[50] Grim and Tucker, *Ecology and Religion*, 86–87.

[51] Ibid., 86.

[52] Ibid., 86–87.

[53] Ibid.

[54] William Braud, "An Introduction to Organic Inquiry: Honoring the Transpersonal and Spiritual in Research Praxis," *The Journal of Transpersonal Psychology* 36, no. 1 (2004): 18.

a sacred ritual; allowing the unconscious to contribute to the research; listening to and sharing multiple stories, including the author's personal story, within the research; engaging in multiple ways of knowing; and letting research be transformative for researcher and audience.[55] In the process of writing this book, I have noticed that I am drawing on many of the techniques of organic inquiry. I have developed a water ritual that I perform at the beginning of each writing session, giving gratitude to water and asking water to speak through my writing.[56] I am paying attention to dreams about water as I write, keeping track of them in my journals and letting them guide my research.

One of the main focal points of this book includes integrating multiple perspectives into my research, including personal experiences (my own and others) and the voices of water. As Clements et al. write, *"The topic of an organic study is rooted in the story of the researcher's own personal experience."*[57] As such, I weave narrative into my account to describe my own experiences of water as well as the experiences of others. Narrative provides a way to represent experiential and cultural perspectives of water. I want to tell the story of water, the multiple stories of the many bodies of water, and narrative is extremely helpful in this endeavor. Thomas Berry gives much inspiration for this narrative approach.

I rely upon organic inquiry throughout this book, and in particular in Chapter 5. In that chapter I share various contemplative practices that engage in multiple ways of knowing water, arguing that such practices can help to transform our

---

[55] Jennifer Clements et al., "Organic Research: Feminine Spirituality Meets Transpersonal Research," in *Transpersonal Research Methods for the Social Sciences: Honoring Human Experience*, ed. William Braud and Rosemarie Anderson (London: Sage Publications, 1998).

[56] I discuss this ritual in Chapter 5.

[57] Clements et al., "Organic Research," 123.

relationship with water. As Clements et al. explain, *"Organic research grows from a reverence for the sacred aspects of the topic, the method, collaboration with the coresearchers, the context, and the implications of the inquiry and may include nonrational and nonverbal ways of gathering and reporting data."*[58] I feel that this work on cultivating an integral water ethic is a transformative process for myself, and I hope that the reader also experiences its transformative potential.

In line with organic inquiry, this book "is grounded in responsibility, reverence, and awe for the earth and all her inhabitants as well as for the mysteries of creativity."[59] In this attitude I explore how water plays a central role within religious myths and rituals, and how contemplative practices with water can transform the ways we know and relate to water. Arising from the encounter of religion and spirituality with water in its many manifestations, an integral water ethic is a guide for cultivating mutually enhancing relations among humans, water, and the entire Earth community.

SIGNIFICANCE

This book has multiple levels of significance—academic, personal, social, and spiritual. It makes a contribution to academic literature by studying water through an integral approach to ecology and highlighting religious, spiritual, and personal perspectives on water. This brings into light how helpful and necessary it is to have a transdisciplinary approach when addressing complex water issues, such as climate change, water pollution, and freshwater scarcity. In highlighting personal and cultural perspectives, I show

---

[58] Ibid., 124.
[59] Ibid., 117.

that subjectivity is an important ingredient that is often overlooked in academic conversations about water and the natural world.

This book has a great deal of significance to me personally. I am a lover of water. I am fascinated with water's beauty, healing qualities, and ubiquitous nature. I'm happiest when I'm in or near water. I love to walk in the rain. I find peace in hearing the sounds of a creek flowing by or seeing the still waters of a lake. I feel awe when I look out at the ocean and see the vast expanse and hear the roaring waves. Waterfalls seem particularly magical. My favorite drink is water. Soaking in hot springs is a special healing treat. Swimming has always been one of my favorite activities, and I have many childhood memories of spending time swimming in pools during the incredibly hot Texas summers. In my mid-twenties I moved to the San Francisco Bay Area and saw the ocean for the first time. The waters of the Pacific Ocean and the San Francisco Bay have since become an incredible source of inspiration for me. I have lived near Strawberry Creek in Berkeley for the past twelve years, and I have found a constant flow of love in this waterway. One of the most sacred places I have come to know is the Esalen Institute in Big Sur, a powerful place where three bodies of water converge: the creek streams through the canyon and flows out into the Pacific Ocean, while hot springs bubble up from the earth and create luxurious healing baths.

This special connection I feel with water calls me to listen to the voices of water and share its messages through my professional work. I wrote my master's thesis on the topic of a philosophy of water through a case study of the Ganges River, focusing on myths and rituals within Hindu traditions that pertain to this aquatic mother goddess, the pollution and damming of the river, and the need for an interdisciplinary approach to bring multiple perspectives together in service of the river.[60] It is my hope that this book is a further step in the development of a philosophy of water, specifically with regards to the ethical relationship between humans and water.

Having confessed that I'm a lover of water, I must confess too that it breaks my heart to see the way humans are treating this precious source of life. The more I become aware of water issues around the world—issues of pollution, overconsumption and desertification, floods and droughts, societies crippled by waterborne diseases, climate change—the more my heart breaks. By writing this book about finding ways to become aware of and concerned for the many voices of water, I am working through the heartbreak and despair that have occurred through becoming educated about the dire state of the world's water. At the same time, this book offers creative ways forward for the future of human-water relations.

In terms of social significance, water is crucial to all societies, and every social structure depends upon water for its sustenance. This book has multicultural significance, as I represent the views of various religious traditions from around the world. I advocate for a democracy of water, which has a threefold meaning: (1) ensuring that humans and all living beings have access to the water they need to survive and flourish, (2) bringing multiple perspectives regarding water into dialogue with one another so that these different perspectives can work together to address pressing water issues, and (3) listening to the voices of water. A democracy of water carries much potential for positive change when it comes to relating to water in sustainable ways.

This book has spiritual significance insofar as it highlights the ways that religious and spiritual traditions have perceived

---

[60] Elizabeth Ann McAnally, "Toward a Philosophy of Water: Politics of the Pollution and Damming along the Ganges River" (MA thesis, University of North Texas, 2007).

water. Interreligious dialogue is necessary for an integral approach to water studies. Perspectives that understand water to be sacred have much to say in the conversation concerning human-water relations, but these perspectives are often left in the background. By considering that water is permeated with vitality and interiority, it is possible to see the material-spiritual forces of the universe at play in the visible world around us.

2

Christianity, Baptism, and Sacramental Consciousness of Water

This chapter explores some of the insights that Christianity has to offer in regard to the cultivation of an integral water ethic. In particular, this chapter explores how baptism, the central ritual of Christianity, can help humans reimagine our relationship with water. I am focusing on the ritual of baptism to see what it might teach us about cultivating a more caring, respectful, and loving relationship with water and with all members of our Earth community.

Some of the main questions I explore in this chapter are as follows: What does baptism symbolize? Where does the water for baptism come from? What happens to the ritual of baptism when water is polluted or privatized? How can baptism assist in reclaiming the importance of materiality? How can the ritual of baptism be an opportunity for raising water consciousness and promoting an integral water ethic? In asking these questions I am working within the context of Christian ecotheology, a field of study that seeks to retrieve ecological insights from Christian texts and rituals and creatively reconstruct them in light of contemporary environmental issues.[1]

One of the main ideas of this chapter is this: by seeing the sacred character of the water of baptism, we can see the sacred character of all water. (This point is elaborated on later in this chapter through the example of Jesus blessing all water when he stepped into the Jordan River to be baptized.) By seeing the fundamental importance of water within Christianity, we can see the fundamental importance of water in our larger Earth community.

In what follows I give an embodied account of baptism to illustrate some of the key features of this ritual. I then explain the theological significance of baptism and provide a brief history of baptism in the early Christian church. I explain how baptism can cultivate a sacramental consciousness, a type of consciousness that celebrates the importance of materiality and the intrinsic value of creation. A sacramental consciousness can promote a reverential care for water and all beings. Furthermore, I explore how situating the ritual of baptism in an ecological context can raise water awareness by linking baptismal waters with the global water crisis and the need for an integral water ethic.

A STORY OF BAPTISM

I was raised in an evangelical Southern Baptist tradition in Texas and have witnessed many baptisms. The following story is my own account of a typical baptism within this

---

[1] For more on ecotheology within the Christian tradition, see John B. Cobb, Jr., *Is It Too Late? A Theology of Ecology* (Beverly Hills, CA: Bruce Publishing, 1972); Sallie McFague, *The Body of God: An Ecological Theology* (Minneapolis: Fortress Press, 1993); Rosemary Radford Ruether, *Gaia and God: An Ecofeminist Theology of Earth Healing* (San Francisco: HarperSanFrancisco, 1992); and Larry L. Rasmussen, *Earth Community, Earth Ethics* (Maryknoll, NY: Orbis Books, 1996).

tradition. I share it here to provide an embodied context for discussing the ritual significance of baptismal waters.

The Southern Baptist preacher and an elementary school-girl are wearing white robes. They are standing in the baptistery, a pool of water about four feet deep that is raised up behind the pulpit at the front of the church. The preacher explains to the congregation that this is a special occasion, a time to celebrate the conversion experience of the child. Just a week ago, while attending a church revival, this young girl asked Jesus to come into her heart and forgive her sins. She has been "born again." By accepting Jesus Christ as her personal Lord and Savior, her old self as a lost sinner has died, and she now has a new life in Christ. The preacher explains that she is coming forward to profess her faith and follow in the next step of her new life as a Christian: baptism. Baptism, the preacher explains, is a symbolic act. The conversion experience happened at the revival. She has Jesus in her heart now. She is saved from hell by the blood of Christ, who died for her sins, and now she is making public her inner experience, coming in front of the congregation and being baptized. Baptism does not save her, the preacher goes on to explain. It is a mere symbol. Becoming baptized is important because it is a way to follow Jesus, just as he was baptized in the Jordan. The preacher now holds a cloth over the girl's nose to prevent the baptismal water from entering it. He says, "I baptize you now in the name of the Father, and of the Son, and of the Holy Spirit." As he lowers her backward and down into the water, he says, "Buried with Christ in believer's baptism." Then lifting her back up out of the water, he says, "Raised to walk in newness of life."

This kind of baptism is called full immersion baptism, wherein the person being baptized is lowered completely under the water by the preacher. It is common among Baptists, Disciples of Christ, and Mennonites. This is also a form of "believer's baptism," which takes place soon after a person makes a profession of faith (that is, "born again" as a believer of Jesus Christ). Baptism, as stated on the Southern Baptist Convention website, "is the immersion of a believer in water" and "an act of obedience symbolizing the believer's faith in a crucified, buried, and risen Saviour, the believer's death to sin, the burial of the old life, and the resurrection to walk in newness of life in Christ Jesus." Believer's baptism differs from the baptism of infants, which involves sprinkling or pouring holy water onto the head of an infant (in some cases the infant is immersed in the holy water of the baptismal font). Infant baptism is common in the Catholic Church and the majority of Protestant denominations, and churches that practice infant baptism also baptize adults when they convert to Christianity and become members of the church.

While churches may vary in the specific way they baptize, they share a central theme: baptism is performed with water. Baptism is dependent upon water. The Greek word for baptism, *baptein*, means "to plunge, to immerse, or to wash."[2] Baptism is thoroughly a water ritual, and it is fundamental to Christians. As Chamberlain notes, "For Christians, the primary ritual is baptism: the death of the old and the rebirth of the new *in the waters*. No other medium so powerfully conveys the meaning of baptism as birth to a new life."[3] Because baptism is the central ritual of the Christian tradition, it follows that water is central to Christianity. As Ecumenical Patriarch Bartholomew of the Eastern Orthodox Church writes in a

---

[2] Michel Meslin, "Baptism," trans. Jeffrey C. Haight and Annie S. Mahler, in *Encyclopedia of Religion*, ed. Lindsay Jones, second ed. (Farmington Hills, MI: Macmillan Reference USA, 2005), 2:779.

[3] Gary L. Chamberlain, *Troubled Waters: Religion, Ethics, and the Global Water Crisis* (Lanham, MD: Rowman and Littlefield Publishers, 2008), 168.

statement on water, "Just as water is the essence of all life, water is also the primary element in the life of a Christian, where the sacrament of Baptism marks the sacred source of the spiritual life."[4] Baptism is fundamental to Christians, and water is a crucial part of the identity of Christians.

THE THEOLOGICAL SIGNIFICANCE OF BAPTISM

Baptism is the central ritual of Christianity. The *Catechism of the Catholic Church* declares the following:

> Holy Baptism is the basis of the whole Christian life, the gateway to life in the Spirit *(vitae spiritualis ianua)*, and the door which gives access to the other sacraments. Through Baptism we are freed from sin and reborn as sons of God; we become members of Christ, are incorporated into the Church and made sharers in her mission: "Baptism is the sacrament of regeneration through water in the word." (no. 1213)

Baptism is a ritual of initiation into the Christian church and faith, and it symbolizes the purification of sins. Just as water cleans the physical dirt from one's body, baptismal waters clean the moral dirt from one's soul. The baptismal waters represent the purification given through Jesus, who called himself Living Water. In his conversation with the Samaritan woman at the well, Jesus said, "Those who drink of the water that I will give them will never be thirsty. The water that I will give will become in them a spring of water gushing up to eternal life"

---

[4] Ecumenical Patriarch Bartholomew, "Statement by His All Holiness Ecumenical Patriarch Bartholomew for the WCC Working Group on Water," August 12, 2005, World Council of Churches, "Water of Life: An Invitation to Participate in the Ecumenical Water Network" (Geneva: World Council of Churches, January 2006).

(John 4:14). Jesus is the Living Water that purifies, and this purification is enacted through the ritual of baptism.

Baptism is the first of the seven sacraments of the Roman Catholic Church and the Eastern Christian Church. The term *sacrament* comes from the Latin word *sacramentum*, meaning "an oath," "bond," or "pledge." *Sacramentum* is the Latin translation of the Greek word *mustērion*, which "is of uncertain etymology but is most probably associated with *muein*, meaning 'to close' (the mouth), and thus 'to keep secret.'"[5] A sacrament can be defined as follows:

> In its classical (Augustinian) meaning, a sacrament is a visible sign of an invisible grace. Paul VI provided a more contemporary definition: "a reality imbued with the hidden presence of God." A sacramental perspective is one that "sees" the divine in the human, the infinite in the finite, the spiritual in the material, the transcendent in the immanent, the eternal in the historical.[6]

As John Hart, a professor of Christian ethics at Boston University, explains, "*Sacraments* are signs of the creating Spirit that draw people into grace-filled moments permeated by a heightened awareness of divine presence and engagement with divine Being."[7] Sacraments are signs of God's grace and are used to enact experiences of the sacred. As Catholic theologians Michael Himes and Kenneth Himes note, "The essence of a sacrament is the capacity to reveal grace, the agapic self-gift of God, by being what it is. By being thoroughly

---

[5] Theodore W. Jennings, Jr., "Sacrament: An Overview," in Jones, *Encyclopedia of Religion*, 12:7954–55.

[6] Richard P. McBrien, "Roman Catholicism [First Edition]," in Jones, *Encyclopedia of Religion*, 12:7881.

[7] John Hart, *Sacramental Commons: Christian Ecological Ethics* (Oxford: Rowman and Littlefield Publishers, 2006), xiv.

itself, a sacrament bodies forth the absolute self-donative love of God that undergirds both it and the entirety of creation."[8] A sacrament reveals God's love by simply being itself. The waters of the sacrament of baptism reflect God's love.

Whether or not baptism is considered to be a sacrament is disputed among the various Protestant Christian traditions. While most Protestant churches consider baptism to be a sacrament, a few denominations (for example, Quakers, Unitarians, and Christian Scientists) do not acknowledge or practice the sacrament of baptism. Other Protestant churches for example, Baptists, Anabaptists, Pentecostals, and Disciples of Christ) practice baptism, but regard it not as a sacrament but as an "ordinance," a ritual ordained or commanded by Jesus. As James V. Brownson, a professor of New Testament at Western Theological Seminary, explains:

> Generally speaking, the word "sacrament" places the focus on baptism . . . as a *means* or *instrument of grace*, a sort of channel through which God's grace comes to us in a unique way. Those who prefer the word "ordinance" emphasize instead that our celebration of baptism . . . is an act of obedience to Christ [and that] God's grace comes always and only through faith in the gospel of Jesus Christ.[9]

When seen as an ordinance, baptism has a more limited symbolic meaning, where the primary focus is having faith in Jesus and undertaking baptism in order to follow Jesus's example. Those who say that baptism is an ordinance often

---

[8] Michael J. Himes and Kenneth R. Himes, "The Sacrament of Creation: Toward an Environmental Theology," *Commonweal* (January 26, 1990), 25.

[9] James V. Brownson, *The Promise of Baptism: An Introduction to Baptism in Scripture and the Reformed Tradition* (Cambridge, UK: Eerdmans, 2007), 22.

argue that baptism itself is not necessary for salvation; rather, it is Jesus who saves, not the baptismal waters. In other words, baptism is a symbolic public act that expresses the pivotal event of accepting Jesus as one's personal Savior. When seen as a sacrament, the act of baptism becomes a necessary and fundamental part of the Christian faith. Baptism as a sacrament has a richer symbolic significance, as it conveys the importance of the material dimension of the ritual: God's grace as the baptismal waters are crucial for salvation. Whether defined theologically as a sacrament or as an ordinance, baptism is an important initiatory act that is dependent upon water.

The precise method of baptism varies across Christian traditions, and at times it even varies within a denomination. As theologian Ian Bradley describes, "There are four main means of Christian baptism: submersion or total immersion of the whole body; partial immersion where the head is dipped under while the candidate is standing in water; affusion where water is poured over the head; and aspersion where water is sprinkled on the forehead."[10] These different methods of baptism highlight different symbolic meanings of water in the New Testament.[11] Immersion baptism enacts the death and resurrection of Christ.[12] As Paul's letter to the Romans states, "Do you not know that all of us who have been baptized into Christ Jesus were baptized into his death? Therefore we have been buried with him by baptism into death, so that, just as Christ was raised from the dead by the glory of the Father, so we too might walk in newness of life" (6:3–4). Going down into the water through total or partial immersion symbolizes death, and coming up out of the water symbolizes birth. In

---

[10] Ian Bradley, *Water: A Spiritual History* (London: Bloomsbury Publishing, 2012), 30.

[11] Brownson, *The Promise of Baptism,* 74–76.

[12] *Catechism of the Catholic Church,* no. 1214.

this way, Christians often refer to baptismal waters as a tomb for the old self and a womb for new life in Christ.

Affusion, or pouring water either by hand or with a special utensil onto the head of the one being baptized, conveys the pouring out of the Holy Spirit into the believer.[13] This is described in Romans as follows: "Hope does not disappoint us, because God's love has been poured into our hearts through the Holy Spirit that has been given to us" (5:5). Aspersion, or sprinkling water by hand onto the head of the one being baptized, invokes cleansing rituals in the Old Testament, which often involved sprinkling water or blood.[14] For example, the prophetic Book of Ezekiel states, "I will sprinkle clean water upon you, and you shall be clean from all your uncleannesses, and from all your idols I will cleanse you" (36:25). Whether through total or partial immersion, affusion, or aspersion, baptism is a ritual where water is used to wash away sins and bring forth a new disciple of Christ. In this sense water acts as a symbol of the purification of the soul.

It is worth noting here that baptism is an act that always involves at least two people: the one performing the baptism, and the one being baptized. Pope Francis brings up the topic of whether a person can self-baptize. He says: "No one can be self-baptized! No one. We can ask for it, desire it, but we always need someone else to confer this Sacrament in the name of the Lord. Because Baptism is a gift which is bestowed in a context of care and brotherly sharing." The pope goes on to say that "throughout history, one baptizes another, another and another. . . . it is a chain. A chain of Grace."[15] Elsewhere the pope mentions that from the time of Jesus, "there is a chain in the transmission of the faith through baptism. And each

---

[13] Brownson, *The Promise of Baptism,* 75–76.

[14] Ibid., 75.

[15] Libreria Editrice Vaticana, "Pope Francis: General Audience: Saint Peter's Square, Wednesday, 8 January 2014."

one of us is a link in that chain! Always moving ahead like a river that flows."[16] Baptism, the defining ritual of Christianity, gives Christians an identity born from water. Each Christian is a drop in the river of the Christian tradition, and the baptismal waters form the aquatic medium of that river.

THE BAPTISM OF JESUS AND BAPTISM
IN THE EARLY CHURCH

The Gospels in the New Testament recount that Jesus was baptized in the Jordan River by his cousin John the Baptist, who "appeared in the wilderness, proclaiming a baptism of repentance for the forgiveness of sins" (Mark 1:4). The ethicist Christiana Zenner Peppard points out that "the baptism of Jesus is one of the few events mentioned in all four gospels of the New Testament."[17] As described in the Gospel of Mark: "Jesus came from Nazareth of Galilee and was baptized by John in the Jordan. And just as he was coming up out of the water, he saw the heavens torn apart and the Spirit descending like a dove on him. And a voice came from heaven, 'You are my Son, the Beloved; with you I am well pleased'" (1:9–11).

Through this event of baptism, the intimate connection among Jesus, God, and the Holy Spirit is made manifest. Baptism reveals the Holy Trinity—God the Father, God the Son, and God the Holy Spirit. As Pope John Paul II explains, "The whole Trinity is therefore present at the Jordan to reveal this mystery, to authenticate and support Christ's mission

---

[16] Catholic News Service, "Pope Francis on the Meaning of Baptism" (January 15, 2014).

[17] Christiana Z. Peppard, "Troubling Waters: The Jordan River between Religious Imagination and Environmental Degradation," *Journal of Environmental Studies and Sciences* 3 (2013): 114. For references to Jesus's baptism, see Matthew 3:13–17, Mark 1:9–11, Luke 3:21–22, and John 1:29–34.

and to indicate that with him salvation history has entered its central and definitive phase."[18] This salvific mission of Christ is continued through baptism. Just as Jesus was baptized, his followers are called to be baptized. In the Great Commission the resurrected Jesus gives his followers this mission: "Go therefore and make disciples of all nations, baptizing them in the name of the Father and of the Son and of the Holy Spirit" (Matt 28:19). By being baptized himself, and by instructing his followers to baptize believers, Jesus gives the model and teaching of baptism.

As Bradley reports, "Full immersion in an outdoor lake or river, with both baptiser and baptised going under the water and rising again, seems to have been the most common means practised in the early days of the church."[19] The simultaneous baptism of a large number of people at once was also common in early Christianity. Acts 2:41 describes a mass baptism of three thousand people.

The *Didache* or *The Teaching of the Twelve Apostles*, an anonymous early Christian text from the second century, describes the type of water that is to be used for baptism:

Now about baptism: this is how to baptize. Give public instruction on all these points, and then "baptize" in running water, "in the name of the Father and of the Son and of the Holy Spirit." If you do not have running water, baptize in some other. If you cannot in cold, then in warm. If you have neither, then pour water on the head three times "in the name of the Father, Son, and Holy Spirit."[20]

---

[18] Pope John Paul II, "General Audience, April 12, 2000."

[19] Bradley, *Water,* 30–31.

[20] Cyril C. Richardson, ed., in collaboration with Eugene R. Fairweather, Edward Rochie Hardy, and Massy Hamilton Shepherd, *Early Christian Fathers*, trans. Cyril C. Richardson (New York: Touchstone, 1996), 174.

The "running water" referred to in the *Didache* is considered "living water." In biblical times "living water" was contrasted with stagnant water. "Living water," as Robin Jensen explains, includes "cold running water in a natural conduit such as a stream or river" and is juxtaposed with "water in ponds, cisterns, ditches, caverns and rain ponds."[21] Hart elaborates on this point:

> As a life-giving and life-providing nourishment, water that is "alive" is water flowing pure and free, and is available in surface rivers, streams, and springs, and from underground aquifers accessed through wells. . . . By contrast, water from pools (constructed to contain diverted flows from springs or streams) and cisterns (plaster-lined underground containers holding rain channeled from roofs, which first were developed in about 1200 BCE) is stagnant and laden with the taste of minerals and of the materials used to confine it.[22]

The *Apostolic Tradition* from the third or fourth century has similar instructions to those of the *Didache* "but indicates that baptisms were being administered in basins that were most likely indoors."[23] Thus, it is generally understood that baptism moved from natural bodies of water to indoor baptismal fonts by the third or fourth century.[24] As Jensen explains, "The very word 'font' *(fons)* denotes a fresh, bubbling spring," but since natural flowing water was not always available, the early church father Tertullian deemed that "any kind of water was permissible provided for such circumstances."[25]

---

[21] Robin M. Jensen, *Living Water: Images, Symbols, and Settings of Early Christian Baptism* (Leiden: Brill, 2011), 133.

[22] Hart, *Sacramental Commons*, 85.

[23] Jensen, *Living Water*, 133.

[24] Ibid., 134.

[25] Ibid., 133.

Tertullian writes, "It makes no difference whether a man be washed in a sea or a pool, a stream or a fount, a lake or a trough," for all waters, "after invocation of God, attain the sacramental power of sanctification."[26]

According to Augustine of Hippo (354–430), baptism is the water and the word of God together. Saint Augustine describes baptism in this way:

> What is baptism? The bath of water with the word. Take away the water, and there is no baptism. Take away the word, and there is no baptism. It is, then, by water, the visible and outward sign of grace, and by the Spirit that the man who was born solely of Adam in the first place is afterwards re-born solely in Christ.[27]

During the Protestant Reformation of the sixteenth century, Martin Luther referred back to these words of Augustine, stating "baptism is not merely by water, but water used according to God's command and connected with God's word," such that when the words of the Great Commission from the end of Matthew's Gospel "are added to the water, then it is no longer simple water like other water, but a holy, divine, blessed, water."[28] In other words, holy water is water that has been blessed by the word of God, traditionally spoken by a priest.

SACRAMENTAL CONSCIOUSNESS AND THE IMPORTANCE OF MATERIALITY

As mentioned above, in the Catholic Church and many Protestant denominations, baptism is considered to be a

---

[26] Tertullian, "On Baptism," trans. S. Thelwall, in *Ante-Nicene Fathers*, vol. 3, ed. Alexander Roberts, James Donaldson, and A. Cleveland Coxe (Buffalo, NY: Christian Literature Publishing Co., 1885).

[27] Saint Augustine, in Bradley, *Water*, 33.

[28] Martin Luther, in ibid., 34.

sacrament, a ritual act that reveals God's grace in the world. Seeing the world with a sacramental consciousness involves seeing the world as a sacrament, sacred, as manifesting the divine. As Hart explains, "A sacramental consciousness is a creation-centered consciousness; it sees signs of the Creator in creation." He goes on to say, "A *sacramental universe* is the totality of creation infused with the visionary, loving, creative, and active power of the Spirit's transcendent-immanent and creating presence."[29] In the sacramental view God is seen as both transcendent (set apart from creation) and immanent (dwelling within creation). In other words, God is present in each part of the world while simultaneously extending beyond the world.

One of the key points that a sacramental consciousness raises is this: matter matters! While the symbolic dimensions of water are important, the materiality of water is just as important. Indeed, without the material substance of the baptismal waters, the symbolic meaning of baptism could not exist. The importance of the natural world and the urgent need to care for it is expressed in this influential statement by Ecumenical Patriarch Bartholomew:

> *It follows that to commit a crime against the natural world is a sin. For human beings to cause species to become extinct and to destroy the biological diversity of God's creation; for human beings to degrade the integrity of the earth by causing changes in its climate, by stripping the earth of its natural forests, or by destroying its wetlands; for human beings to injure other human beings with disease; for human beings to contaminate the earth's waters, its land, its air,*

---

[29] Hart, *Sacramental Commons*, xviii.

and its life, with poisonous substances—all of these are sins.[30]

By making this connection between environmental destruction and sin, Patriarch Bartholomew is condemning such destructive behavior and encouraging a worldview wherein humans care for the natural world as God's sacred creation.

Sacramentality can play a significant role in promoting care for the material world. As Catholic theologian Catherine Vincie states, "A sacramental theology suggests that God can be and is revealed, embodied, and communicated through created reality." She goes on to say, "sacramentality at its best demands that we take seriously our own materiality and the materiality of our ritual objects."[31] In other words, sacramentality demands that Christians care for not only the ritual symbolism of baptism, but also the physical waters that are fundamental for the ritual to take place. The materiality of the baptismal waters is of crucial importance.

Sacramentality demands that Christians care for creation, for it is through creation that God reveals Godself. Timothy Robinson, a divinity professor at Texas Christian University, explains it like this: "The sacramental significance of water helps us see the vital interconnection among living things that depend upon its material reality for survival and flourishing. It suggests the care of the Creator for the creation and the potential for divine encounter in *this* life, in *this* world."[32]

---

[30] John Chryssavgis, ed., *Cosmic Grace, Humble Prayer: The Ecological Vision of the Green Patriarch Bartholomew*, rev. ed. (Grand Rapids, MI: Eerdmans, 2009), 221.

[31] Catherine Vincie, *Worship and the New Cosmology: Liturgical and Theological Challenges* (Collegeville, MN: Liturgical Press/Michael Glazier, 2014), 85, 86.

[32] Timothy H. Robinson, "Sanctified Waters: Toward a Baptismal Ethic of Creation Care," *Leaven* 21, no. 3 (2013): 164.

Sacramentality can help shift the focus of care from an after-life in heaven to the work that must be done here on Earth in this present moment.

WATERS OF BAPTISM, WATERS OF LIFE

Sacramental consciousness expands one's consciousness to see that all water has the potential to be a sacrament and provide access to God. As Mary Dodge writes:

> Sacramentality is the vision that sees the reflection of all the Earth's water in the baptismal font, water that flows in our oceans, lakes, and rivers, water that lays deep underground trying to survive pollution, and water that pours from faucets to clean and refresh us. Catholic sacramental worldview is the foundation for my assertion that it is meaningful to envision the water of baptism as symbolic of the Earth's water.[33]

Seeing baptism as a sacrament through a sacramental consciousness can lead to seeing all waters as sacred and deserving of respect and care. Dodge goes on to explain:

> The water of baptism is not merely a disposable symbol that mechanistically connects humans to a higher reality; it has intrinsic value and points to the reality that all water is holy. It offers a sign that, through baptism, people enter into an Earth-honoring Christian faith. It signifies that the earth-human community is inextricably connected because water is the substance that sustains every member.[34]

---

[33] Mary Dodge, "All Water Is Holy: Ecological Catechesis for Baptism" (PhD dissertation, St. Thomas University, 2015), 23.

[34] Ibid., 8.

This connects back to the point that materiality matters. Baptismal waters are not simply about symbolic meaning divorced from materiality. Baptism in full symbolic meaning includes the physical dimension of the baptismal waters. As Robinson puts it, "The material substance used as a sign of God's grace in baptism is drawn from that same water upon which all living things depend for survival."[35] It is literally the case that the waters of baptism are the same waters that flow in the church's watershed. The waters of life that are represented through the act of baptism are the same waters of life that come out of the faucet or flow in a local creek.

Furthermore, some Christians argue that all waters were consecrated by Jesus's baptism in the Jordan. As McDonnell notes, the Syriac poet-theologian Jacob of Serugh (451–521) "is explicit in saying that by stepping down into the Jordan Jesus consecrated all waters: 'The entire nature of the waters perceived that you had visited them—seas, deeps, rivers, springs and pools all thronged together to receive the blessing from your footsteps.'"[36] By stepping into the Jordan and being baptized in these waters, Jesus blessed all waters. It is important for those of us alive today to remember this point. According to the Christian tradition the waters that we interact with on a daily basis have been blessed through Jesus's baptism. A sacramental view of baptism can help to awaken a deeper appreciation for all water and can motivate Christians to not pollute, privatize, or otherwise desecrate the water that Jesus made sacred.

As stated above, Pope Francis explains that baptism is a river or chain that links all Christians together. In this way baptism forms a water lineage that connects Christians to

---

[35] Robinson, "Sanctified Waters," 160.

[36] Kilian McDonnell, *The Baptism of Jesus in the Jordan: The Trinitarian and Cosmic Order of Salvation* (Collegeville, MN: The Liturgical Press, 1996), 61.

the Trinity (God the Father, God the Son, and God the Holy Spirit), as well as to the community of believers who have been baptized. The baptismal water lineage also connects Christians to all waters on Earth. Through baptism, Christians have their identity rooted in water. This aquatic identity extends beyond Christians to include all people and all life forms. For water gives us life. Water makes us who we are. We are water beings living in a water world.

SACRAMENTAL WATERS
AND THE I-THOU RELATION

As an agent in the world, water nourishes all life on Earth when it is allowed to flow freely and be clean. When viewed with a sacramental consciousness, water manifests compassion, divinity, and care. As Hart explains: "Living water is a sacramental commons in itself. It is sacramental when its purity symbolizes divine being, divine compassion, and divine solicitude, and provides nourishment for all life."[37] Living water is a commons when it is able to support and nourish all life. Living water is sacramental when it reveals God's grace.

Ecotheologian Larry Rasmussen discusses the importance of a sacramental consciousness for water ethics. Seeing water as a sacrament includes recognizing the intrinsic value of water:

The basic ethical reorientation commended here belongs to an eco-spirituality that includes a profoundly sacramental sense. Water is the object of awe and not *only* the object of engineering; it is the medium of the mystical and not *only* a resource for a world of our own

---

[37] Hart, *Sacramental Commons*, 91.

making; water is a "thou" and not *only* an "it." . . . It's worthy of reverence.[38]

Here Rasmussen is drawing from Martin Buber (1878–1965), the Jewish existentialist philosopher who articulates two primary modes of relationship: "I-Thou" and "I-It."[39] Water is not only an "it," a resource for humans to use and treat as an object. Water has much more than mere instrumental value; water has the intrinsic value of simply being what it is. Humans can enter into an I-Thou relationship with water, which entails a reciprocal relationship based on love. As Buber writes, "Love is responsibility of an I for a You."[40] God reveals Godself uniquely through water, just as God reveals Godself in other ways through other aspects of creation. Because water is part of the creation of the divine, an expression of God's divinity and grace, and a mode through which humans can relate to God, water is worthy of respect, care, and reverence. Relating to water as a You or Thou is an encounter with the wholly other mystery that manifests in the form of water.

As mentioned above, Himes and Himes define a sacrament as having the ability to reveal God's grace and love "by being what it is," by simply being itself. Furthermore, they say, "By its nature a sacrament requires that it be appreciated for what it is and not as a tool to an end; in Buber's terms, a sacrament is always 'thou.'" The sacramental vision "provides the deepest foundation for reverencing creation," for "every creature, human and non-human, animate and inanimate, can

---

[38] Larry L. Rasmussen, *Earth-honoring Faith: Religious Ethics in a New Key* (New York: Oxford University Press, 2013), 282.

[39] Martin Buber, *I and Thou*, trans. Walter Kaufmann (New York: Touchstone, 1970).

[40] Ibid., 66.

be a sacrament."[41] Through a sacramental consciousness, all waters are sacramental. As such, no body of water can be treated as a mere tool for human use. Water must have the freedom to be itself, to flow freely for all beings.

WHEN BAPTISMAL WATERS
BECOME POLLUTED AND PRIVATIZED

What happens when water is treated a mere means and not an end in itself? In particular, what does an instrumentalist attitude do to the sacramental character of water? For example, what happens to the ritual of baptism when water is polluted or privatized? John Hart has some helpful insights about this issue. The global water crisis, Hart notes, reflects a critical shift: "Earth's waters have become less sacramental, less a revelatory sign of the Spirit's presence and creativity, and more detrimental, more signs of human ignorance, carelessness, indifference, and greed." When water is polluted, he writes, "It no longer has a sacramental character as a sign in nature of the Creator Spirit." This is because the impurities of the polluted water "hide and dilute the essence of the pristine water that once flowed as a sign of the Creator's artistry, solicitude for life, and immanence in creation."[42]

Hart goes on to say, "The symbolism of the ritual would be subverted by the use of polluted water in the sacramental moment—and might well endanger the health or even life of the recipient of the sacrament. The person spiritually bathed in, blessed by, and cleansed through such water would be distracted from appreciating its spiritual significance because of its polluted material condition."[43] Polluted waters could distract, harm, or even kill the one being baptized. Pure, clean

---

[41] Himes and Himes, "The Sacrament of Creation," 25, 27, 27.
[42] Hart, *Sacramental Commons*, 91, 80, 80.
[43] Ibid., 90.

water is essential for the ritual. The emphasis in the early Christian church on the use of "living water" for baptism (as opposed to stagnant water) reflects this point.

The sacramental character of water is also negatively affected in light of the current widespread trend of water privatization. Hart reflects, "When water is *privatized*, it is prevented from providing freely to living beings its life-giving nourishment. . . . When water is privatized, its sacramental role in the commons is denied to many. Its availability as a sign of a loving Spirit who cares for all life is limited." Using privatized water for baptism would diminish the sacramental character of the ritual. In this case "water intended for all would be available for spiritual cleansing only to the extent that its 'owners' allowed it to be so allocated. Water would not be a sign of God's providence (to meet human subsistence needs) and God's freely given grace (to guide human spiritual needs) if its use were dependent on private whim."[44]

When the waters of baptism are compromised in light of pollution or privatization, the efficacy of baptism is compromised. Hart notes, "The waters of baptism could not signify spiritual cleansing and entrance into a new life in an inclusive, integrated community if water used for the sacrament were polluted periodically and/or only secured sporadically from an exclusive, elitist group's restricted private source."[45] Water must be kept clean and pure and accessible to all people in order for baptism to have the full possibility of its meaning.

Peppard draws on Hart's work in her analysis of the pollution of the Jordan River: "One might therefore infer that the pollution and degradation of the Jordan would—or at least, should—be of particular concern to Christians. Thus far, however, there has been little Christian ethical engagement with the waters of the Jordan." She notes the parallel between

---

[44] Ibid., 80, 90.
[45] Ibid., 90.

the Jordan and the Yamuna rivers of northern India: "In both cases a polluted, degraded river nonetheless both signifies and confers a type of purity. Is it possible that the material and symbolic status of the river might be drawn together more tightly than at present?"[46]

In response to Peppard's question I hold that a sacramental view of baptism has the potential to integrate the material and symbolic dimensions of water. When baptism is viewed with a sacramental consciousness, it is possible to regard all water as a holy gift of God that we are called to care for and love. By polluting and privatizing waters we damage our relationship with God and creation, as these denigrated forms of water obscure the divine body of God, the manifestation of divinity within the world. By viewing water as a sacrament, as a manifestation of God's grace, it is evident that our relationship to water reflects our relationship to God. Thus, caring for water is a way to care for God.

BAPTISM, WATER CONSCIOUSNESS, AND WATER ETHICS

The ritual of baptism can be used as an opportunity to raise water consciousness and cultivate an integral water ethic. Rituals are potent with significance, and, as Chamberlain explains, "ritual practices are vital resources for developing a new consciousness around water and new commitments for action. For Christians, the primary ritual is baptism: the death of the old and the rebirth of the new *in the waters*."[47] What if baptism were situated in an ecological context? What if those who are being baptized were instructed to care for the waters of creation? Leaders in the Association of African

---

[46] Peppard, "Troubling Waters," 118.
[47] Chamberlain, *Troubled Waters*, 168.

Earthkeeping Churches (AAEC) are doing just this, integrating ecology and ethics in the ritual of baptism:

> In the baptismal context they started to insist that converted novices not only confess their moral sins in relation to fellow human beings but also their *ecological sins*: felling trees without planting any in return, overgrazing, riverbank cultivation, and neglect of contour ridges, with soil erosion as a result—in other words, taking the good earth for granted and exploiting it without honoring or nurturing it.[48]

In this model baptism "required the new convert's commitment to active participation in restoring creation as part of God's plan and as a sign of genuine conversion in recognition of the gift of God's free grace."[49] Genuine or authentic conversion includes a change of heart in all aspects of one's life, including how one relates to the natural world. Spiritual conversion must include ecological conversion.

In his papal encyclical *Laudato Si': On Care for Our Common Home*, Pope Francis argues for the need for an ecological conversion, through which "the effects of their encounter with Jesus Christ become evident in their relationship with the world around them. Living our vocation to be protectors of God's handiwork is essential to a life of virtue; it is not an optional or a secondary aspect of our Christian experience" (no. 217). Pope Francis goes on to explain that an ecological conversion facilitates an understanding that the "world is God's loving gift" and that humans are to have a "spirit of generous care" for the world and cultivate values of gratitude

---

[48] Marthinus L. Daneel, "African Initiated Churches as Vehicles of Earth-Care in Africa," in *The Oxford Handbook of Religion and Ecology*, ed. Roger S. Gottlieb (New York: Oxford University Press, 2006), 546–47.

[49] Ibid., 547.

and generosity and an awareness of the interconnectedness of humans with the world (no. 220). Ecological conversion would respond to issues of global inequality, capitalism and consumerism, and the well-being of the poor, for "a true ecological approach *always* becomes a social approach; it must integrate questions of justice in debates on the environment, so as to hear *both the cry of the earth and the cry of the poor*" (no. 49). With the phrase "the cry of the earth and the cry of the poor," Pope Francis is referring to the work of the Brazilian liberation theologian and integral ecologist Leonardo Boff.[50]

Robinson explores how baptism can cultivate water ethics, or what he calls a "baptismal eco-ethic." He asks this question: "is not the baptized person—and the community of the baptized—obligated to 'die to the sin' of ecological degradation, overconsumption, and the unjust appropriation of resources?"[51] Robinson argues:

> The ethical imperative of baptism includes responsible action toward other-than-human creatures and ecosystems so that the will of God for the flourishing of the whole creation might be realized. Baptism in water, water drawn from the earth's lifeblood, connects us intimately to the material elements upon which humans and all living beings depend for survival. The sacramental connection between the birth, life, death, and resurrection of Jesus and the material elements that function for us as signs of God's saving and sanctifying work in Jesus set forth a moral vision for the Christian life that includes attentive care for the earth and just distribution of its resources.[52]

---

[50] Leonardo Boff, *Cry of the Earth, Cry of the Poor*, trans. Phillip Berryman (Maryknoll, NY: Orbis Books, 1997).

[51] Robinson, "Sanctified Waters," 161, 164.

[52] Ibid., 165.

In other words, the baptismal eco-ethic that Robinson illustrates is grounded in the sacramental connection between baptismal waters and the waters of the world outside the church, which have both material and symbolic significance. Christian water ethics includes care of water and water justice.

Rachel Hart Winter, an ecotheologian, shares her reflections on how the ritual of baptism can assist in raising water consciousness:

> In the celebration of this rite I see an immense opportunity for education and increasing awareness about the water crisis. Baptism is a valuable moment in which the theology of water might be linked to our ethical imperative to care for it as part of God's creation. The reference to a baptismal cleansing where God is praised for the water to "cleanse and give new life" could have profound implications for how we understand the necessity of this resource for both physical and spiritual nourishment.[53]

She goes on to say, "There are 2 billion Christians around the globe. Imagine if we harnessed the moment where each one of those people is baptized to create an ethical command for protecting our waters." She invites the reader to imagine baptisms without water, or baptisms that are held in waters unsafe to drink or bathe in. "The reality of unclean water for one third of our global population offers an excellent entry point for Christian ethics." She continues: "Stories of those who suffer due to the water crisis connected with a baptismal call to become like Christ would not fall on deaf ears to those who are participating in and witnessing to the sacrament."[54]

---

[53] Rachel Hart Winter, "Water for Alinglaplap; Visions of Water from Alinglaplap," *@ this point* 10, no. 2 (2015).

[54] Ibid.

In response to Winter's essay, Martha Moore-Keish offers ideas for practical ways to heighten awareness of the ethical responsibility humans have to water. She mentions that stories of those who are suffering in light of the global water crisis could be shared in sermons or teachings surrounding baptism. She also suggests bringing awareness to the use of local waters in the font or baptistery and making explicit the connection between the baptismal waters and the local watershed of the church. In addition, she advocates for baptisms being held in local bodies of water like a lake, stream, or bay. These types of actions can "draw attention to the material reality of water, and can stimulate gratitude as well as concern for its use."[55]

The call to raise water consciousness through baptism is also encouraged by Mary Dodge, who notes that this concern helped to motivate her dissertation research:

> As a religious educator for many years, I catechized hundreds of parents seeking baptism for their children. . . . Looking back with my wider view of how this commitment [of parents to raise their children in the Christian faith] extends to honoring all that God has created, I realize I could have included in that conversation an appreciation of the critical link between the water in the font, water in the world beyond the church doors, and clean water shortage in many parts of the world. My current awareness of the absence of this catechesis motivates this project as I question whether baptism preparation is an opportunity to transform our relationship with water.[56]

If water awareness could be raised during baptismal rituals, this could have positive implications for the protection of

---

[55] Martha Moore-Keish, "Author's Response," in ibid.
[56] Dodge, "All Water Is Holy," 9.

water. By linking baptismal water with the waters that flow throughout one's local watershed and the larger world, Christians can be encouraged to practice viewing all water as holy water. The cultivation of a sacramental consciousness can help Christians to extend their reverence for God and their reverence for baptismal water to a reverence for all water and all of creation. Thus, a sacramental consciousness of baptism can assist in the cultivation of an integral water ethic that cares for all waters and all beings.

The sacrament of baptism can be remembered and celebrated throughout one's life as a way of renewing one's relationship to God and water. Pope Francis has emphasized that it is important for Christians to both know and celebrate the day that they are baptized. During his General Audience in St. Peter's Square on January 8, 2014, the pope said, "Do not forget your homework today: find out, ask for the date of your Baptism. As I know my birthday, I should know my Baptism day, because it is a feast day." Pope Francis noted that many Christians are baptized as infants and have no recollection of their baptism. Therefore, it is important for Christians to celebrate the day that they are baptized so that they can actively remember this holy sacrament and renew their vow to follow Christ. The pope explained in the General Audience,

> To know the date of our Baptism is to know a blessed day. The danger of not knowing is that we can lose awareness of what the Lord has done in us, the memory of the gift we have received. . . . We must reawaken the memory of our Baptism. We are called to live out our Baptism every day as the present reality of our lives.

The gift of God's grace is enacted through baptismal waters. Thus, the anniversary of one's baptism could be reimagined as a type of water birthday. On the yearly anniversary of their baptisms, Christians could perform various types of water-related service or scholarship: picking up trash in local creeks and along the coast; learning more about their water identity and their kinship with others through water; exploring the connections among domestic use, industrial agriculture, factory farms, and the overconsumption and pollution of water; and renewing their vows to be like Christ through caring for those marginalized, especially those without access to clean water or improved sanitation. The yearly celebration of one's baptism is a way to remember the inherent connection between the waters of baptism and the waters of daily life and thus to renew one's care for water as a manifestation of God's grace.

CONCLUSION

This chapter explored how baptism can help us uplift the value of water and transform our relationship with water and our Earth community. Baptism is a water ritual that is at the center of the Christian faith. Baptism can be employed as a teaching tool to help raise water consciousness and water ethics, thus transforming our relationship with water and our Earth community. Baptism is a potent moment in the life of the one being baptized, in the life of his or her family, and in the church community. Baptism reflects a conversion experience, a change of heart. The sacrament of baptism has the possibility for awakening not only a spiritual conversion but also an ecological conversion. If the Christian experience of spiritual conversion can be more explicitly connected with ecological conversion (as is happening in the African Earth-keeping Churches), this could have profound implications for addressing the global water crisis. The act of following Christ through baptism can be translated as an act of following

Christ's example of caring for all creation. Thus, the spiritual and potentially ecological conversion moment of baptism could inspire Christians to take practical steps in addressing issues of water pollution, privatization, freshwater scarcity, access to clean drinking water and improved sanitation, and climate change.

Drawing together awareness of the waters in the baptismal font or baptistery and the waters of the world can help Christians have a more intimate relationship with water. Showing the inherent intertwinement of the symbolism of water (as cleansing, purifying, transforming, and generating) and the materiality of water can help us awaken our consciousness and help us have a more intimate relationship with our world. Baptism is a tool for awakening a sacramental consciousness. It is a way into seeing the sacredness of the world. Viewing baptism as a sacrament and seeing water as a sacred mirror reflecting God's grace can help us see how the whole world can be a sacrament and a way to connect with the divine.

Crucial to the Christian faith is the belief that Jesus Christ died, was buried, and was resurrected. As Jesus called himself Living Water, we could draw from this imagery and reinterpret the resurrection of the Living Water as a call to resurrect the physical waters of our local watersheds. Resurrecting waters could mean cleaning up pollution and reviving the life-giving waters so that water is no longer dead (without oxygen) but is vibrant and alive so that life forms can flourish. Resurrecting waters could also mean literally bringing water above ground, "daylighting" creeks that have been put in culverts underground.

Resurrecting water brings water into our consciousness and our ethical concern. This would entail not only cultivating a more intimate personal relationship with water, but also responding to the systemic ecological sin related to the industrial growth society and capitalism, which sees water as a mere resource and commodity whose primary role is to generate profits for the rich at the expense of the poor and the Earth community. An integral water ethic holds that we need to pay attention to water, not to take water for granted but instead to show respect and care for this source of life. Resurrecting water means cultivating a sacramental consciousness, so that we see the sacred present in the world around us. The holy waters of baptism are part of the same hydrological cycle that flows throughout the world.

Viewing water through a sacramental consciousness would help us not to take water for granted, not to waste the precious water of life. It would also help us to have more gratitude and wonder at the preciousness and mystery of water. Can we learn to see the ordinary water of the faucet as the extraordinary waters of life? We need to make the connection that all water is sacramental and worthy of attentive reverence. Through the sacrament of baptism, we can learn to have a deeper communion with water and all beings.

3

Hinduism, the Yamuna River, and Loving Service of Water

The Yamuna River flows through northern India for approximately 855 miles, from its source at the Yamunotri Glacier in the Garhwal region of the Himalayan Mountains in the state of Uttarakhand to its confluence with the Ganges River in the city of Allahabad. From this point, the Yamuna and the Ganges flow together as one river (called the Ganges or Ganga), nourishing the fertile plains of India with the rich sediment they carry from the Himalayas and flowing out the Bay of Bengal to the Indian Ocean. Throughout its course the Yamuna is fed by a number of tributaries: Tons, Chambal, Sindh, Betwa, and Ken. Furthermore, the Yamuna is the principal tributary of the Ganges. Approximately 60 million people in India depend upon the Yamuna's waters for survival.[1]

The Yamuna River has been revered by Hindus throughout history as a sacred river that is the aquatic embodiment of Yamuna, the goddess of love. While this river is still worshiped today, it has become intensely polluted in the past few

---

[1] Richard Conniff, "The Yamuna River: India's Dying Goddess," *Environment YALE* [Journal of the Yale School Forestry and Environmental Studies] (Spring 2011).

decades because of rapid industrialization. In response to this pollution a number of Hindu environmental activists in India have reinterpreted religious myths and practices to provide motivation to restore the health of the river.

In this chapter I consider the relevance of the Hindu concept of *seva* (loving service) for an integral water ethic. I first give a brief description of the Yamuna River, tracing its flows in India. I then provide accounts of sacred perceptions of the river found within Hindu myths, scriptures and poetry, and rituals and practices. Following this, I describe the current ecological state of the river, noting various threats to the vitality of the river and those who depend upon it. I then explore religious responses to the degradation of the river. I conclude with some reflections of how this case study is applicable to the development of an integral water ethic.

TRAVELING TO INDIA:
ABOVE AND BELOW THE CLOUDS

During the winter of 2010–11, I traveled to India for a month-long journey through the country. As a doctoral student researching integral water ethics, I had been invited to participate in a conference on the Yamuna River. Flying into New Delhi, I could see out the window the long range of the Himalayan Mountains in the distance. The mountains were magnificent and grand, the sky clear and sunny. Large fluffy white clouds gathered below to form a dense cushion. The scene outside the window was picturesque.

During our plane ride the flight attendants served bottled water labeled Mount Kailash. For me, this was ironic. So much intersected in this bottle of water: the name of a mountain that is sacred in many of the religious traditions of Asia (including Buddhism, Hinduism, Bon, and Jainism); the commodification of water (the source of life demoted to a profitable resource); the misleading trend of bottled water companies to make the water seem more appealing by connecting it to a pure, untouched source (the water in this particular bottle was not extracted from the watersheds of Mount Kailash; instead, the fine print on the label noted that this water came from deep bore wells in Anangpur, Faridabad, Haryana near New Delhi); and the vast amounts of pollution connected with the production, distribution, and the disposability of single-use plastic bottles.[2] Given the vast complexity of ecological and social justice issues surrounding bottled water, I was disturbed that the sacred mountain of Kailash was used for marketing purposes.

As I drank this water and contemplated the irony of sacred water in plastic bottles, the plane began to descend below the fluffy white clouds and the scene changed completely. The clear, blue, peaceful sky was replaced with a very dark, smoggy, gray sky. The view below provided a miniature glimpse of an industrial-growth society. Before my eyes I saw two worlds juxtaposed: a seemingly pristine world above and a heavily polluted world below. I had just been contemplating Mount Kailash and the paradox of putting sacred water in a plastic bottle for a profit, and the new scene felt surreal.

When we landed in New Delhi and I stepped off the plane, my first reaction was, "What is burning?" It seemed to me that the whole city must be on fire. My travel companion assured me that there was no raging fire; this was the smell of intense air pollution. I was shocked and horrified. I had known that New Delhi is one of the most polluted cities in the world.[3] However, experiencing this pollution firsthand was a different

---

[2] For more about the social and environmental impact of bottled water, see Peter H. Gleick, *Bottled and Sold: The Story behind Our Obsession with Bottled Water* (Washington, DC: Island Press, 2010).

[3] Patralekha Chatterjee, "India Takes Steps to Curb Air Pollution," *Bulletin of the World Health Organization* 94 (2016): 488.

thing altogether. I was amazed that this was normal for the residents. As someone who has suffered from asthma for most of my life, I was greatly saddened to think of how this poor air quality was negatively affecting the well-being of the people who call India their home. As the World Health Organization reports, air pollution is the "world's largest single environmental health risk" and is "a major risk factor for heart disease, stroke, chronic obstructive pulmonary disease (umbrella term for several progressive lung diseases including emphysema) and lung cancer, and increases the risks for acute respiratory infections and exacerbates asthma."[4] Breathing the polluted air while I was in India helped me feel within my body how critical this issue is.

YAMUNA RIVER CONFERENCE

I traveled to India not to study air pollution but rather to do research about the polluted rivers of India, rivers that have been revered as goddesses but are also intensely polluted. The primary reason for my travels to India was to participate in an interdisciplinary conference entitled "Yamuna River: A Confluence of Waters, a Crisis of Need."[5] This conference was held January 3–5, 2011, and was organized by the Yale Forum on Religion and Ecology and co-sponsored by Yale University and TERI University in New Delhi. The purpose of the conference was to bring together a group of diverse scholars and activists from India and the United States to dialogue about the Yamuna River. *Confluence* was included in the conference title as a water metaphor for the convergence of multiple perspectives. Approximately twenty people were invited by Yale and TERI University to participate in the

---

[4] Ibid., 487.

[5] For more about this conference, see "Yamuna River Conference," http://fore.yale.edu/yamuna-river-conference/.

conference, including scientists specializing in toxicology, hydrology, chemistry, microbiology, and ecology, as well as environmental engineers, political scientists, anthropologists, scholars of religious studies, local religious leaders, and representatives of local nongovernmental organizations.

The conference resulted in the "Yamuna River Declaration," in which participants committed to the following: (1) continuing scientific research at TERI University and Yale University about the ecology, hydrology, and biology of the Yamuna; (2) supporting conservation projects and educational initiatives in religious settings; and (3) sustaining interdisciplinary dialogue that "brings together diverse communities along the Yamuna River so that voices, projects, and aspirations might be articulated regarding scientific research and religious education concerning water usage and water ethics."[6]

The first half of the conference was held at TERI University in New Delhi in an academic setting where participants gave presentations related to the Yamuna River. The second half was held in Vrindaban at Jai Singh Ghera, the ashram of Shrivatsa Goswami, where there was public discussion among the conference participants, the community members of Vrindaban, nongovernmental organizations, and religious leaders. While we were there, we also observed the river firsthand and witnessed religious rituals related to the river.[7]

We convened at this conference to engage in dialogues about the current condition of the Yamuna River and potential actions that might be beneficial for its future flow. Those of us gathering at the conference did so because of our mutual concern about this particular river. The Yamuna River acts

[6] John Grim and Mary Evelyn Tucker, *Ecology and Religion* (Washington, DC: Island Press, 2014), 198–99.

[7] For more about the Yamuna River Conference, see ibid., 140–53, 197–99.

as a confluence of different perspectives. It is considered to be one of India's most sacred rivers, yet at the same time it is one of the most polluted rivers in the world. The story of the Yamuna is described in detail by religious scholar David Haberman in *River of Love in an Age of Pollution*.[8] In this chapter I highlight some of key themes that Haberman explores in depth so that I can then draw out useful concepts for an integral water ethic.

One facet of the story of the Yamuna that I find especially helpful for developing such an ethic is the movement currently emerging in India that is motivated by the Hindu concept of *seva* (loving service) for the ecological restoration of the river. As Haberman notes, "A few decades ago, *seva* would have referred specifically to 'loving service' that took the form of standard acts of worship, such as making offerings of hymns, flowers, fruit, milk, and incense." He explains that a cultural transformation has been recently taking place, and "although the word still retains the older meaning, increasingly it includes actions that we in the West would label 'environmental activism.'"[9] Indeed, ecological restoration of the river is currently being enacted by a number of Hindus as a form of religious devotional service. This is important to me because love is a crucial component of an integral water ethic. Love can be a powerful motivation to engender the protection and restoration of waterways. This case study of the Yamuna River is a helpful example in which we can see how love has motivated environmental restoration. I share this example with the hope that it can inspire others to interact with local waters with an attitude of loving service.

---

[8] David L. Haberman, *River of Love in an Age of Pollution: The Yamuna River of Northern India* (Berkeley and Los Angeles: University of California Press, 2006).

[9] Ibid., 179.

SACRED PERCEPTIONS OF THE YAMUNA RIVER

The Yamuna River is considered by Hindus to be one of the most sacred rivers of India, revered as "an aquatic form of divinity for thousands of years" and understood to be "a divine goddess flowing with liquid love."[10] Widely venerated as a goddess, Yamuna plays an important role in Hindu myths and rituals.

The Yamuna River is believed to be the liquid embodiment of the goddess Yamuna, the divine mother who nourishes her children with her life-giving waters. She purifies the sins of those who bathe in her waters, liberating them from death. In Braj, the cultural region in Uttar Pradesh, India, which includes the cities of Mathura and Vrindavan, Yamuna worship has been sustained for many centuries. In this region, Yamuna is known by many names: "Mother of the World, Highest Divinity, Supreme Lover of God, Ultimate Giver, Perfecter of Love, Purifier of All, Daughter of the Sun, and Sister of Death."[11] In Hindu mythology Yamuna is the daughter of Vivasvat (Brilliant One), who is also known as Surya (Sun), and his wife Samjna (Consciousness). Yamuna's elder twin brother is Yama, the god of death. The goddess Yamuna is also known as Yami and Kalindi.

It is said that Yamuna lived in heaven until seven great sages prayed that she descend to Earth so that she could help "develop the devotional insight *(bhakti)* of the living."[12] In response to the sages' prayers, Yamuna flowed down from heaven onto Mount Kalinda in the Himalayas, forming cascades of beautiful waterfalls as she flowed down the mountain. Because she began her course in such a cold region, Yamuna was afraid that many people would not make

---

[10] Ibid., 1.
[11] Ibid., 107.
[12] Ibid., 45.

pilgrimage to her source. Thus, she prayed to her father, the sun god, to make her earthly setting more attractive. So the sun shined bright and caused a ray of his light to strike a rock at the base of the waterfall, causing boiling water to appear as a natural hot springs. Thus, the frigid waterfall and the hot springs at the glacier Yamunotri are together the source of the Yamuna River.[13] The sound of the boiling water that gushes out of the rock is interpreted by the Yamunotri priests to be the voice of one of the seven sages, Jayamuni, who is praising Yamuna, whose name is also Kalindi, by chanting "Kalindi namah" ("All glory to Kalindi").[14]

Yamuna devotees make pilgrimage to Yamunotri to bathe in these pleasurable hot springs. A small tank has been built to hold some of this sacred hot springs water, known as Surya Kund (Pond of the Sun), where pilgrims can take a ritual bath.[15] They often cook rice in these waters by using a cloth and string to tie together a bag and place it in the hot waters, eating it as *prasad*, a gracious edible gift from the goddess to be ritually consumed. In many pictures and paintings at Yamunotri, Yamuna is depicted riding a turtle as she sits on top of a lotus:

> She is four-armed, holding a pot in her upper left hand, a lotus flower in her lower left hand, and a string of medi-tation beads in her lower right hand, and she displays the fear-not gesture with her upper right hand. . . . The symbols of the bountiful pot and creative lotus make it evident that Yamuna Devi is a powerful goddess who manifests life-giving forces and blessings.[16]

---

[13] Ibid., 46.
[14] Ibid., 52.
[15] Ibid., 53.
[16] Ibid., 55.

Yamuna is the chief lover of Krishna, the youthful god who entrances cowherd maidens with his divine flute music. The river is the flowing stream of liquid love between Krishna and Yamuna. Her waters are said to be full of her erotic relationship with Krishna. The Ashta Chap, a group of eight famous Indian poet-saints of the sixteenth century, wrote forty-one poems about Yamuna that form the foundation for much of Yamuna theology.[17] One poem by Govindaswami describes the river this way: "Her flow of drops of love sweat rushes toward her beloved ocean."[18] In another poem Rasika Pritama (the pen name for the commentator Hariray) writes, "She flows with divine sweat produced from blissful lovemaking."[19]

The sounds of Yamuna's water are interpreted as sacred sounds full of love for Krishna. Her waves are said to be the sound of her voice chanting the name of her beloved Krishna, "Hari, Hari."[20] The rushing river sounds "are interpreted as the jingling of anklets on her running feet" as she hurries to her lover.[21] The poet and commentator Hariray explains that the "sounds of the babbling stream are her love songs as she moves excitedly toward Braj." While Yamuna is depicted riding a turtle at her source in the Himalayas, she is often shown running to Krishna in images in Vrindaban.[22]

Yamuna is a "goddess of exquisite love and compassion . . . who experiences the deepest of all loves, and who, rather than holding onto that love for herself, shares it selflessly with all who approach her with an open heart."[23] Her water flows

---

[17] For these forty-one poems, see Haberman, *River of Love in an Age of Pollution*, 202–15.

[18] Ibid., 203, 261n8.

[19] Ibid., 203, 260n5.

[20] Ibid., 220.

[21] Ibid., 117.

[22] Ibid.

[23] Ibid., 104.

from the heart of Vishnu Narayana, the infinite god connected with the sun, and thus embodies the liquid love *(rasa)* of the god.[24] Many believe that worshiping Yamuna brings the devotee into union with Krishna. This belief is reflected in this line of "Shri Yamuna Chalisa," a poem by Pannalal Purushottam Shastri: "Whoever performs loving service [*seva*] to you, O Yamuna, is united with the young King of Braj [Krishna]."[25]

Numerous religious rituals take place in this river and along its banks. As Haberman describes, people come into contact with the goddess through acts of worship that include "bathing in a religious manner, reverently touching or sipping the water, meditating on Yamuna's divine form, or simply gazing at the aquatic form of their goddess and thereby experiencing a visual communion *(darshan)* with her."[26] Bathing in the holy waters is traditionally seen to be extremely beneficial and purifying. In the *Padma Purana*, a Hindu religious text, it is said that "all minor and major sins are reduced to ashes by taking a bath in Yamuna."[27] Yamuna is the sister of Yama, the god of death, and it is believed that bathing in the river will prevent suffering in hell. As it is said in the "Yamunotri Mahatmya" of the Hindu text *Skanda Purana*, "One who bathes here in the Yamuna even once does not go to the realm of Yama, but achieves the highest goal."[28]

THE CURRENT CONDITION
OF THE YAMUNA RIVER

While the Yamuna River is revered as a holy goddess in the Hindu tradition, its physical waters are severely threatened. The river has extreme pollution caused by agricultural

---

[24] Ibid., 117, 128, 240.
[25] Ibid., 217. Brackets in the original.
[26] Ibid., 104.
[27] Ibid., 59.
[28] Ibid., 58.

pesticides and herbicides, toxic industrial wastes, and human biological wastes; at the same time, the river lacks a robust flow due to dams and the over-extraction of water for irrigation.[29] To better understand these issues, it is helpful to look at various segments of the river.

Upstream, as the Yamuna River flows freely from the Yamunotri glacier, the waters are pristine. However, as the river leaves the Himalayas and enters the plains, it is heavily managed. At the town of Dakpathar in Uttarakhand, a giant concrete barrage (diversion dam) has been constructed over the river, and much of the water is diverted into canals for hydroelectric power production. The river is further managed as the water flows through another barrage in the Yamuna Nagar district of the state of Haryana. The Hathni Kund Barrage (which replaced the Tajewala Barrage) divides the Yamuna into the Western and Eastern Yamuna Canals, where the waters are channeled for irrigation to such an intense extent that only 10 percent of the waters of the Yamuna flow on downstream to New Delhi.[30] Before and after Delhi the river passes through two more barrages, one at Wazirabad, upstream of Delhi, and another at Okhla, in South Delhi.

Delhi, a megalopolis whose population in 2018 rose to 27,928,000 people,[31] is on the banks of the Yamuna and "is by far the greatest contributor to Yamuna pollution. Although it covers only 2% of the river's length, Delhi produces more than 70% of the pollution load in the river."[32] In Delhi, the

---

[29] Conniff, "The Yamuna River."

[30] Haberman, *River of Love in an Age of Pollution*, 5, 7.

[31] "Delhi Population 2018," http://worldpopulationreview.com/world-cities/.

[32] Haberman, *River of Love in an Age of Pollution*, 76. Haberman's book was published in 2006. The Centre for Science and Environment notes that in 2009, the amount of pollution from Delhi had increased to over 80 percent. Centre for Science and Environment, "State of Pollution in the Yamuna" (2009), 1, http://indiaenvironmentportal.org.in/files/State%20of%20the%20Yamuna_0.pdf.

Yamuna River is transformed into a sewer, as over half of the human sewage in Delhi is directly released into the river with no treatment, resulting in "fecal coliform counts in places reaching over 100,000 per 100 milliliters (200 times the standard for water to be swimmable)."[33] In June 2001, volunteers removed thirty-six truck-loads of trash from the Yamuna River in Delhi in a mere five days.[34]

The river is ecologically "dead" as it flows through Delhi. The amount of organic pollution in the river, signified by the biochemical oxygen demand (BOD), is much greater than the level of dissolved oxygen (DO) in the river. Indeed, eutrophication (extreme oxygen depletion) is taking place, as the DO level is zero in Delhi. As Haberman explains, "The Yamuna rapidly becomes asphyxiated in Delhi; it literally can no longer sustain life."[35] Environmentalist Sunita Narain describes it in the following way: "Yamuna through Delhi is not a river. The definition of a river is that it must have life and how you measure life is that it must have capacity to dissolve oxygen. And the dissolved oxygen content in Yamuna as it passes through Delhi is zero. Which means it's dead. . . . It just hasn't been officially cremated."[36]

The flow of the river is greatly decreased due to over-extraction for agricultural irrigation. Only a small percent of water extracted for irrigation is returned to the river. Thus, there is little to no water left in the river to dilute the waste. The Indian Supreme Court proclaimed in July 2000 that "Yamuna is only a drain which resembles a river in the monsoons and remains a drain for the rest of the year."[37]

---

[33] Conniff, "The Yamuna River."

[34] Haberman, *River of Love in an Age of Pollution*, 168.

[35] Ibid., 81.

[36] In Ketki Angre, "Yamuna: A River That's All but Dead," NDTV (March 15, 2013).

[37] Haberman, *River of Love in an Age of Pollution*, 167.

Furthermore, climate change is posing a threat to the Yamunotri glacier, the source of the river. If this glacier and others in the Himalayas continue to recede, the source of water for the people of India and throughout Asia will be seriously threatened.[38]

RELIGIOUS RESPONSES TO THE DEGRADATIONOF THE YAMUNA RIVER

What does this pollution of the Yamuna River mean for Hindus? How does the pollution affect the religious views of Yamuna devotees? The answer to these questions depends on who is responding. Haberman notes three distinct responses from Yamuna devotees in Braj regarding the modern pollution of the river:

> Some denied that the pollution has any real effect on the river goddess or on living beings dependent on her; some acknowledged that the pollution harms living beings who come in contact with the water but does not affect the river goddess herself; and some contended that the pollution is having a harmful effect on beings who come in contact with the water as well as on the river goddess herself.[39]

These three groups hold differing views of the characteristics of Yamuna as a mother goddess. According to the first group, pollution does not negatively affect the goddess, humans, or other living beings—"Yamuna is an all-powerful

---

[38] Deepika Aggarwal and J. S. Pasricha, "Climate Change and Its Impacts on Indian Agriculture," *International Journal of Climate Change: Impacts and Responses* 2, no. 3 (2011): 163.

[39] Haberman, *River of Love in an Age of Pollution*, 133.

Mother" who always "takes care of her children no matter how naughty they are."[40] This type of response often resists or is indifferent to environmental efforts to clean the river, as the all-powerful river goddess is believed to take care of herself and her children. As Haberman explains, this view is "based on a feminine theology that tends to view the river goddess in a highly transcendent fashion."[41] Here we see a transcendent divinity whose purity is unaffected by physical pollution. As one boatman on the river tells Haberman: "Yamuna-ji is never polluted. Her water is pure."[42]

This transcendent view of a river goddess is further explored by anthropologist Kelly Alley in the context of the Ganges River, another sacred river of India that is severely polluted with urban sewage, industrial waste, and ritual practices for the dead, including dispersing cremated ashes into the river and immersing corpses.[43] As Alley explains, many who live in Varanasi, India, as well as those who go there to make pilgrimage, "claim that Gaṅgā, like a good mother, cleans up after the messes her children make and forgives them lovingly. In this way, she cleans up other kinds of dirtiness people bring to her, excusing them with maternal kindness."[44] They distinguish between material cleanness and ritual purity, reporting that "Mother Gaṅgā could unfortunately become unclean *(asvaccha* or *gandā)*, but that she could never be impure *(aśuddha* or *apavitra)*," for the Ganges River "is a goddess who possesses the power to absorb and absolve

---

[40] Ibid., 138.

[41] David L. Haberman, "How Long Is the Life of Yamuna-ji?" paper for The Yamuna River: A Confluence of Waters, a Crisis of Need workshop (January 3, 2011), 4.

[42] Haberman, *River of Love in an Age of Pollution*, 134.

[43] Kelly D. Alley, *On the Banks of the Ganga: When Wastewater Meets a Sacred River* (Ann Arbor: University of Michigan Press, 2002), 51.

[44] Ibid., 64–65.

human and worldly impurities."[45] Environmental activists in Varanasi, Alley reports, argue that this understanding of the "sacred purity and loving tolerance" of the Ganges River often "leads to a passive acceptance of polluting behavior."[46]

Returning to Haberman's account of the three different views of Yamuna as a mother goddess, those in the second group also consider Yamuna as an omnipotent mother who herself cannot be changed by physical pollution, but these devotees believe that pollution can harm humans and other living beings. They understand pollution-related diseases and deaths to be the punishment of the goddess. Haberman recounts a conversation with a young priest in Vrindaban, who explains: "Mother Yamuna gives us back whatever we give her. If we give her good things, we get back good things. If we give her bad things, then she gives us back bad things. Therefore, for our sake we should stop polluting her."[47] Another account of this view is stated as follows: "Pollution cannot affect the supernatural. For those who can see this, Yamuna-ji is a pure goddess. She cannot be polluted. But we are not supernatural. We are natural. Therefore, it is us who will suffer from the pollution."[48] This second group is more likely than the first to engage in environmental efforts, but not to the extent of those in the third group.

Devotees in the third group view "Yamuna as an ailing Mother who is herself affected by the pollution and who is

---

[45] Kelly D. Alley, "Separate Domains: Hinduism, Politics, and Environmental Pollution," in *Hinduism and Ecology: The Intersection of Earth, Sky, and Water*, ed. Christopher Key Chapple and Mary Evelyn Tucker (Cambridge, MA: Harvard University Center for the Study of World Religions, 2000), 357.

[46] Kelly D. Alley, "Idioms of Degeneracy: Assessing Ganga's Purity and Pollution," in *Purifying the Earthly Body of God: Religion and Ecology in Hindu India*, ed. Lance E. Nelson (Albany: State University of New York Press, 1998), 312.

[47] Haberman, *River of Love in an Age of Pollution*, 136.

[48] Ibid.

in need of the loving care of her devotees."[49] In this way the maternal theology of the Yamuna "can now work both ways, evoking either a self-nurturing presence or a presence in need of care herself."[50] This third group emphasizes the immanent nature of the divine over its transcendent character, holding that physical pollution has a negative effect on the health of the divine. This is expressed by one Vrindaban holy man: "If you destroy the river, Yamuna-ji is finished! The river is the real goddess, not some lady sitting on a turtle."[51] Here we see that the goddess Yamuna cannot be separated from the physical river.

This worldview is also held by Gopishwar Nath Chaturvedi, a traditional ritual leader for pilgrims who is widely known in Braj for his efforts to clean the Yamuna River. In 1985, while he was leading pilgrims to the Yamuna for a ritual bath, Chaturvedi saw that the river was polluted with red and blue industrial dyes dumped by nearby mills and that dead fish covered the riverbanks. "This scene struck him as a desecration of his mother, the river Yamuna."[52] The experience affected Chaturvedi deeply and motivated him to engage in legal work in the courts, filing public interest litigation (PIL) that resulted in the High Court of Allahabad imposing a ban on the release of untreated sewage and industrial effluents into the river by the end of December 1999.[53] He says: "Mother is very sick. When one's mother is sick, one does not throw her out of the house. We must help her. Therefore, I do Yamuna *seva*."[54] Haberman explains that when Chaturvedi talks

---

[49] Ibid., 138.

[50] Ibid., 137.

[51] Ibid., 139.

[52] Vasudha Narayanan, "Water, Wood, and Wisdom: Ecological Perspectives from the Hindu Traditions," *Daedalus* 130, no. 4 (2001): 193.

[53] Haberman, *River of Love in an Age of Pollution*, 143.

[54] Haberman, "How Long Is the Life of Yamuna-ji?" 5.

of Yamuna *seva*, he does so in a way that signifies both his spiritual worship of the river as well as his environmental work to clean the river.

> He said that *seva* now means both worshipping *(puja karna)* and environmental protection *(paryavaran surak-shan)*. . . . *Seva* in this context is environmental action understood and expressed as a form of religious devotion. It is usually performed out of strong sentiment or love *(bhava,* to use the religious word) for a particular form of divinity, in this case Yamuna.[55]

The eco-spiritual movement drawing on the concept of Yamuna *seva* is growing in India. Vrindaban priest Govinda Sharma says, "Yamuna-ji is in danger! We must all perform *seva* [loving service] to save her and make her free from pollution."[56] One very popular sign in Vrindaban has this message: "Mother Yamuna has given so much. Now Yamuna asks for loving service [*seva*]."[57]

Seva is also a concept invoked by Veer Bhadra Mishra, the late *mahant* (chief priest) who was head of the Sankat Mochan Hanuman Temple and the Swatcha Ganga (Clean Ganga) Campaign in Varanasi, India. He says: "People worship Ganga as a goddess, or simply as 'Ma.' We work *for her*."[58] Mishra has a deep sense of love of the Ganges River. He urges people to employ the energy of love in protecting and cleaning the river. In doing so, he makes a strong case for the need to be empathetic to the perspective of others and to speak to others in ways that resonate with their worldview. As an article in the *New Yorker* reports:

---

[55] Haberman, *River of Love in an Age of Pollution,* 180.
[56] Ibid., 150. Brackets in the original.
[57] Ibid., 162. Brackets in the original.
[58] Ibid., 183.

The mahant is also convinced that science and religion have to mesh if the Ganges is to be saved. The Western approach, based on fear of a possible ecological disaster, will not work, he said. "If you go to people who have a living relationship with Ganga and you say, 'Ganga is polluted, the water is dirty,' they will say, 'Stop saying that. Ganga is not polluted. You are abusing the river.' But if you say, 'Ganga is our mother. Come and see what is being thrown on the body of your mother—sewage and filth. Should we tolerate sewage being smeared on the body of our mother?' you will get a very different reaction, and you can harness that energy."[59]

Mishra and others thus reflect upon the importance of talking with devotees first and foremost in terms of their faith, and in doing so, arousing a sense of duty to care for the divine mother through religiously motivated environmental actions.

Furthermore, invoking a fear of disaster is not the most effective way of relating to devotees. Haberman notes, "Religious love is a strong motivation for environmental activism in India, which fairly well distinguishes it from the dominant form of environmental activism typically found in the United States."[60] This is a crucial point to consider in light of environmental efforts in a larger context. Could love, instead of fear, be a more useful way to motivate others to engage in environmental and social efforts? Haberman thinks so, and I agree. He says:

Love builds and goes somewhere—perhaps like a river—whereas fear might foster greater denial and serve to dam up effective action. The Yamuna devotee

---

[59] Alexander Stille, "The Ganges' Next Life," *The New Yorker* (January 19, 1998), 65–67.

[60] Haberman, *River of Love in an Age of Pollution*, 180.

Vasishthagiri told me, "The way to tap into the infinity of love is to give it infinitely. It flows like a river but becomes stagnant when it is stopped, dammed, or held onto out of fear or selfishness."[61]

Fear is reactionary and constricting. It is a conditional response—"Because this is happening, I am afraid." Fear tends to produce a fight, flight, or freeze response. As Haberman notes, fear can be counterproductive and can lead to denial of the problem. On the other hand, love is open and unconditional. Love is infinite and infinitely accessible. Love is unlimited and generates more love. Love is not attached to an outcome but gives itself freely.

I find it very helpful to look to water as a model for cultivating loving service. Water can teach us how to love if we imitate its flow. As the famous Indian environmental activist Sunderlal Bahuguna puts it:

Living in the company of nature, one learns many things. This river here flows for others. It is a model of loving service [*seva*]. Have you ever seen a river drinking its own water? Thus, nature sets an example for us human beings, and says that, if you want real peace and happiness, be in close contact with me. Living rivers give us so much.[62]

Learning to see water as a model for loving service is at the heart of an integral water ethic. Water is a teacher and guide. We can learn to love water by witnessing how water expresses love for living beings, flowing in service of the health of others.

---

[61] Ibid., 183–84.

[62] Sunderlai Bahuguna, in Haberman, *River of Love in an Age of Pollution*, 72. Brackets in Haberman.

Religious myths are being retold and reinterpreted in light of the pollution of the Yamuna River. There is a famous myth of Krishna saving the Yamuna River from pollution.[63] It comes from the *Bhagavata Purana*, one of the most significant religious texts in Braj culture. Haberman says that this story is told often in speeches about the pollution of the Yamuna River. The story goes as follows:

The many-headed poisonous serpent Kaliya came to the Yamuna River and began to reside there in a deep pool. His presence caused the river to become poisoned. Trees on the riverbank died, birds flying over the river immediately died and fell out of the sky, and Krishna's cowherd friends and their cows drank the water and became very sick. When Krishna realized that these calamities were due to the poison of Kaliya, Krishna fought the serpent, wrestling him in the water for two hours. Finally Krishna overcame Kaliya, and he climbed on top of the serpent's many heads and began a death dance on them. Kaliya surrendered and pleaded for mercy. Krishna relented and demanded that the serpent leave Braj and never return. Thus, the river was restored, animals and plants came back to life, and the cowherds were revived.

This popular story in Hindu mythology has new significance in light of the current pollution of the Yamuna River and is increasingly shared to invoke loving service for the river. "The poison comes not from a mystic serpent, but from the factories and sewers of Delhi, seventy miles upstream."[64] The people of Braj say that the poison of the serpent Kaliya now manifests as "the drains discharging domestic and industrial wastes into the river, that the various pipes are his many

---

[63] Ranchor Prime, *Hinduism and Ecology: Seeds of Truth* (Delhi: Motilal Banarsidass Publishers, 1994), 97, 115–16; Haberman, *River of Love in an Age of Pollution*, 150–51.

[64] Prime, *Hinduism and Ecology*, 116.

poisonous heads."[65] This myth helps to instill a sense of moral duty for cleaning the pollution of the river. As Bahuguna says:

This pollution [of the present day] is the Kaliya snake and every citizen has to play the role of Krishna today. That means you have to become like Krishna—a lover of all life; at one with the universe. Until then you cannot save this river from being polluted; you cannot save this world from being exploited by the demons like Kaliya.[66]

Becoming like Krishna by bringing love to the center of one's life is a powerful way to motivate efforts to clean up the river.

Shrivatsa Goswami, one of the most important and well-known of the Radha Raman *goswamis* (priests) in Vrindaban, India, also draws from the inspiration of Krishna in his efforts to restore the health of the Yamuna River. Goswami says that Krishna is the "ecological guru" and that Krishna's life is "the greatest chapter in environmental history."[67] The two main aspects of Krishna's environmentalism are "repairing environmental damage and worshipping nature."[68] Furthermore, as Goswami says: "The ultimate aim of Krishna is to establish the human value of love. Love is the key to all sustainable living."[69] Through a deep love of Yamuna, devotees can find inspiration and strength to engage in environmental efforts as an act of *seva* to the divine.

There is concrete evidence that *seva* has produced positive results for the restoration of the Yamuna River. Hinduism and

---

[65] Haberman, *River of Love in an Age of Pollution*, 150.

[66] Bahuguna, in Prime, *Hinduism and Ecology*, 97.

[67] Haberman, *River of Love in an Age of Pollution*, 155; Prime, *Hinduism and Ecology*, 54.

[68] Haberman, *River of Love in an Age of Pollution*, 155.

[69] In ibid., 157.

ecology scholar Bidisha Mallik notes that in 1998 religious leaders and pilgrims held protests against the pollution of the Yamuna that have been effective, resulting in court mandates to check the pollution of the river.[70] Furthermore, in 2010, the Braj Vrindavan Heritage Alliance was formed to protest arbitrary development on the river and prevent the construction of an overpass over the Yamuna near Keshi Ghat.[71] In addition, in March 2013 the Yamuna Rakshak Dal (Save Yamuna Group) led "one of the biggest protests against river pollution in India," a massive march consisting of 20,000 to 100,000 protestors that began in Vrindaban and marched 85 miles to Delhi. Radha Kant Shastry, one of the organizers of the march, explained that "our two key demands are that Yamuna should be allowed to flow unrestricted and that the Delhi's polluted water should not flow into the Yamuna."[72] These examples, as well as the public interest litigation by Chaturvedi described above, provide evidence that *seva* is an effective motivating force for environmental restoration of the Yamuna.

In this vein South Asian religion professor Bruce Sullivan explains that "many Hindus are skeptical of scientific justifications for ecological programs and might be more receptive to programs that have religiously sensitive approaches and religiously significant outcomes."[73] He further makes the connection between devotional service to Krishna and environmental restoration: "Those who are most devoted are

---

[70] Bidisha Mallik, "Science, Philosophy, and Policy on the Yamuna River of India," *Environmental Ethics* 36, no. 3 (2014): 297.

[71] Ibid., 298.

[72] Hari Kumar, "Massive March for Yamuna River Nears Delhi," *New York Times* (March 11, 2013).

[73] Bruce M. Sullivan, "Theology and Ecology at the Birthplace of Kṛṣṇa," in *Purifying the Earthly Body of God: Religion and Ecology in Hindu India*, ed. Lance E. Nelson (Albany: State University of New York, 1998), 261.

taking the lead in the environmental cleanup of Braj. And for those who have not yet matured in their devotion, the beautification of the environment may be an aid to devotional practice. Certainly it can be regarded as service of Kṛṣṇa and an appropriate way of caring for Kṛṣṇa's creation."[74]

Vasudha Narayanan, who is widely known for her scholarship in Hinduism and ecology, echoes this point of the importance of devotional religious sentiments in Indian environmentalism. She writes, "Devotional *(bhakti)* exercises seem to be the greatest potential resource for ecological activists in India. As we have seen, devotion to Krishna or to Mother Ganga or Yamuna has impelled some people to take action to supply safe drinking water, plant and protect trees, and clean up rivers."[75] Devotion to manifestations of the divine within the physical world is a powerful tool for evoking ecological responsibility within Hindu devotees.

AN INTEGRAL WATER ETHIC AND YAMUNA *SEVA*

As I argue throughout this book, an integral approach to water is needed for a flourishing future. This means that religion needs to be in dialogue with ecological science and policy to effect lasting change. The "Yamuna River Declaration" that resulted from the Yamuna River conference in which I participated makes this point as well:

Unique among world rivers, the Yamuna and several other Indian rivers are revered as Goddesses in the living Hindu tradition. We wonder, therefore, if there might be a way for devotees of the river to integrate a deeper sense of environmental awareness and conservation into their religiosity. Thus, pollution could be

---

[74] Ibid., 258.
[75] Narayanan, "Water, Wood, and Wisdom," 202.

mitigated through environmental engagement as a loving and respectful relationship with the river. Are there not new and creative ways to bring scientific research on the river together with the transformational power of religious devotion? The life of the river may depend on such a synergy of efforts.[76]

A relationship with the Yamuna based on loving service that is inspired by religious insights and ecological knowledge is crucial to the health of the river. As Haberman concludes from his fieldwork in India, "Yamuna's devotees suggest that we need to respond with love to the now-damaged world in which we live, specifically a love accompanied by an ongoing awareness and appreciation of the wondrous divinity of the world as we sustain a well-grounded and life-affirming commitment to stop human-caused environmental destruction."[77] The waters of the Yamuna, as of all such revered rivers, bear eloquent witness both to the destructive force of humanity and of its struggle to love the world and bring harmony among the divine, the human, and the elemental.

The story of the Yamuna River is important in the context of an integral water ethic because it provides insight into how love can be a motivating force for eco-spiritual efforts to restore waterways. Love is a universal value among all religious and spiritual traditions. Love can be an unlimited source of spiritual energy. The more love one gives others, the more love one has available to give to others.

In the context of Hinduism, love and devotion to the divine are intimately interconnected. As religious-studies scholar Gavin Flood explains, devotional worship *(pūjā)* became very popular in India throughout the first millennium CE; "Performing *pūjā* is a way of expressing love or

---

[76] In Grim and Tucker, *Ecology and Religion*, 198.
[77] Haberman, *River of Love in an Age of Pollution*, 194.

devotion *(bhakti)* to a deity in some form, and became the central religious practice of Hinduism." Devotional love emphasizes "the body, the emotions and the embodied forms of the Lord which could be seen and worshipped." Love in this context entails "an immediate experience of the divine" and becomes the "devotee's emotional outpouring for his or her deity and the sense of losing the limited, self-referential ego in an experience of self-transcending love."[78] Loving the waters of the Yamuna River is a devotional act of worship wherein the devotee's love unites with the infinite love of the goddess. When the ecological restoration of the Yamuna River is performed as Yamuna *seva*, devotional love for the goddess is enacted through practical ways of caring for her liquid flowing waters.

Seva is an approach that has advantages over a strictly utilitarian approach that aims to restore the river for human benefits and health through technical means. A utilitarian approach does not address the need to care for water on the basis that water has intrinsic value (that is, because water exists, it is valuable). Instead, a utilitarian perspective views water primarily in terms of instrumental value (that is, water is valuable because of its economic value and use to humans). This perspective holds that humans should take care of water because the health of water is good for humans. Bad water quality negatively affects humans, and a polluted body of water causes economic loss because people cannot harvest fish from it or enjoy water-related recreational activities. A utilitarian perspective does not focus on the health of the water, the health of the fish, or the health of the ecosystem.

An approach based on *seva*, on the other hand, is "a river-centered approach rather than a human-centered approach."[79]

---

[78] Gavin Flood, *Introduction to Hinduism* (Cambridge: Cambridge University Press, 1996), 103, 133, 131.

[79] Haberman, *River of Love in an Age of Pollution*, 182.

In the example of the Yamuna, loving service is enacted for the river, the mother goddess. Care for the river is not enacted primarily for the good of humans, but instead for the good of the divine river. Yamuna *seva* is first and foremost devotional service to the river goddess whose embodiment is the waters of the river. *Seva* is an approach that ties together values rooted in religious myths, scriptures, and rituals and has the potential to motivate devotees to act in environmentally responsible ways, for devotion to the goddess Yamuna is devotion to the Yamuna River that flows through northern India.

The Yamuna River is regarded by many priests, villagers, and environmentalists as a river goddess of love who is of service to humans and the ecosystems of northern India, and who requests that her devotees practice *seva* and restore her polluted waters. The river itself provides a model for embodying *seva*. As noted above, Bahuguna says that Yamuna is "a model for loving service" because it "flows for others."[80] Recalling Haberman's words, Yamuna is a "goddess of exquisite love and compassion . . . who experiences the deepest of all loves, and who, rather than holding onto that love for herself, shares it selflessly with all who approach her with an open heart."[81] The waters of the Yamuna are an example of the selfless nature of all water, as water gives of itself freely and flows in service of all beings. By witnessing the loving service of water as it provides life-giving sustenance for the Earth community, we discover a model of how to act in loving service for water and all members of Earth. The case of the Yamuna offers a perspective of how even severely polluted waters deserve

---

[80] Bahuguna, in ibid., 72.
[81] Haberman, *River of Love in an Age of Pollution*, 104.

human love in the form of ecological restoration. By cleaning the polluted waters of the Yamuna, and by restoring the health of other bodies of water that are at risk around the world, we have the potential to enact devotional service to liquid manifestations of the divine.

4

Buddhism, Bodhisattvas, and Compassionate Wisdom of Water

In this chapter I explore an integral water ethic in the context of Mahāyāna Buddhism. To do this, I look to the traditional Buddhist image of the bodhisattva, a being who vows to attain enlightenment so that he or she can better benefit others and liberate them from suffering. I then consider how the image of the bodhisattva is taught and embodied through the ecological efforts of the Seventeenth Gyalwang Karmapa Ogyen Trinley Dorje, the Tibetan Buddhist leader. The aim of this chapter is to illustrate how an integral water ethic can be cultivated through Buddhist values of compassion (*karuṇā*) and wisdom (*prajñā*), which some teachers call the two wings of the *dharma*, or the Buddhist spiritual path.[1] Like a bird that needs two wings in order to fly, the Mahāyāna Buddhist path depends on both compassion and wisdom.

---

[1] The term *dharma* has many meanings. For the definition of *dharma* as the path, see Butön Rinchen Drup, *Butön's History of Buddhism in India and Its Spread to Tibet: A Treasury of Priceless Scripture,* trans. Lisa Stein and Ngawang Zangpo (Boston: Snow Lion, 2013), 18.

Further, I explore how the values associated with the bodhisattva, who aims to live in service to others through a deep cultivation of compassion and wisdom, can contribute to an integral water ethic. The intense suffering caused by the numerous water crises throughout the world—associated with climate change, pollution, water scarcity, water-borne diseases, the lack of access of water to the poor—calls for wise and compassionate responses, not only technocratic "fixes" determined by purely political and economic considerations. By learning to practice compassion, we can learn to open our eyes to what is going on around and within us, to open our ears to the cries of suffering, to open our hearts to others who are in need. By skillfully engaging with the suffering of others in our own experience of suffering, we become both more empathic and more equipped to move through suffering together with all those who suffer.

In order to understand the significance of the Mahāyāna concept of compassion and therefore its applicability to environmental issues, it is important to understand its relationship to wisdom, the other wing of the *dharma*. In Buddhism, wisdom entails both an intellectual understanding and a profound experiential realization that all things are deeply interdependent, indeed empty (*śūnya*) of any "self" understood as existing all on its own. Individual beings and the worlds that we share in common are completely intertwined, and the primordial nature of the mind is its emptiness (*śūnyatā*) of any inherently existing self that is separated from the web of being. The qualities of this primordial nature of mind, unlocked through realization of emptiness, are expressions of the natural compassion at the heart of every sentient being. The Buddhist teaching of the interdependence of all things implies the radical insight that the suffering of others is one's own suffering (and vice versa).

Cultivating the wisdom of emptiness thus encourages Buddhist practitioners to act responsibly, with a mindset to benefit others for all the generations to come. Adding to that, I claim that wisely recognizing that water is a substance that flows throughout the world and provides life-giving sustenance for all sentient beings can facilitate a deep understanding and vivid experience of interdependence, and can help us better comprehend that the way we interact with water affects and reflects all of life. This comprehension empowers compassion, which further inspires the cultivation of wisdom. The two ideas of wisdom and compassion are thus inextricably interrelated in Buddhist thought and spiritual practice and are significant for an integral water ethic.

Before going further, it is important to note some criticisms of previous attempts to derive an environmental ethic from Buddhism. Buddhist scholar Ian Harris offers critiques in his essay "Buddhism and the Discourse of Environmental Concern." The central contention of Harris's essay is this: "Supporters of an authentic Buddhist environmental ethic have tended toward a positive indifference to the history and complexity of the Buddhist tradition."[2] He reminds the reader that Buddhism is not a monolithic tradition but is instead a complex tradition full of "historical, doctrinal, and cultural diversity."[3] He writes, "The generalization of ideas or practices from one historical, geographical, or cultural phase of the tradition, in an attempt to justify some monolithic Buddhist position, will be largely illegitimate."[4] He

---

[2] Ian Harris, "Buddhism and the Discourse of Environmental Concern: Some Methodological Problems Considered," in *Buddhism and Ecology: The Interconnection of Dharma and Deeds,* ed. Mary Evelyn Tucker and Duncan Ryūken Williams (Cambridge, MA: Center for the Study of World Religions and Harvard University Press, 1997), 378.

[3] Ibid., 381.

[4] Ibid., 381–82.

says, "It would be unwise to claim, as do many exponents
of an environmentally engaged Buddhism, that Buddhism
contains the intellectual and practical resources necessary
to counteract the adverse effects of modernity."[5] He notes
the philological problems of attempting to equate the Western notion of "nature" with a Buddhist term.[6] Furthermore,
while many examples exist of Buddhists acting in ways that
are ecologically responsible, one can also find examples
of Buddhists acting in ways that are anti-ecological (for
example, deforestation in China during the ninth century).[7]
Harris concludes, "Clearly there are difficulties involved
in translating Western environmentalist discourse into an
authentically Buddhist setting or, indeed, in calling on Buddhism to provide a rationale for ecological activity. This
does not mean that the task is hopeless. I, for one, remain
optimistic about the outcome."[8]

I share Harris's optimism, and I attempt to avoid the
problematic tendencies within Buddhism and ecology that
he elucidates. In what follows I consider textual resources
within the Mahāyāna Buddhist tradition that illuminate the
ecological implications of the bodhisattva archetype. I also
highlight the environmental efforts of a particular Buddhist
leader, the Seventeenth Karmapa, who himself is well-trained
in the history and complexity of the Buddhist tradition. I do
not try to articulate a "monolithic Buddhist position" but
instead draw out ways that Mahāyāna Buddhist texts and an
environmentally engaged Buddhist leader can contribute to
an integral water ethic.

---

[5] Ibid., 387.
[6] Ibid., 378–79.
[7] Ibid., 386.
[8] Ibid., 396.

THE ARCHETYPE OF THE BODHISATTVA AND THE PHILOSOPHY OF WISDOM AND COMPASSION

A bodhisattva is someone who is full of love and compassion for all beings, generating awareness of the suffering of others, including humans, animals, plants, rivers, stones, and other beings, and striving for their well-being. The word *bodhisattva* means a "being (SATTVA) intent on achieving enlightenment (BODHI)."[9] Enlightenment is an awakening to the interdependent and impermanent nature of reality, a realization that the self is empty of independent existence and is instead intimately intertwined with others. The compassionate bodhisattva continually vows to liberate those who are suffering and help them to awaken to the interdependent nature of reality.

The bodhisattva aims to cultivate *bodhicitta*, "the intention to reach the complete, perfect enlightenment . . . of the buddhas, in order to liberate all sentient beings in the universe from suffering."[10] *Bodhicitta* has both a relative aspect and an absolute aspect: relative *bodhicitta* is compassion (*karuṇā*), and absolute *bodhicitta* is wisdom (*prajñā*).[11] According to the *Prajñāpāramitā Sūtras*, "A bodhisattva mahāsattva [great being] is one who strives like this: 'By all means, I shall awaken to unsurpassable enlightenment and accomplish the welfare of

---

[9] Robert E. Buswell, Jr., and Donald S. Lopez, Jr., *The Princeton Dictionary of Buddhism* (Princeton, NJ: Princeton University Press, 2014), 134.

[10] Ibid., 130.

[11] For more about relative *bodhicitta* and absolute *bodhicitta,* see Dilgo Khyentse, *The Heart of Compassion: The Thirty-seven Verses on the Practice of a Bodhisattva,* trans. Padmakara Translation Group (Boston: Shambhala, 2007), 106–74.

others.'"[12] Cultivating the combined wisdom and compassion of *bodhicitta* is the chief practice of the bodhisattva.

Various qualities of bodhisattvas are elaborated in *Bodhicharyāvatāra (The Way of the Bodhisattva)*, a revered manual for the practice of bodhisattvas composed in the eighth century by the renowned Indian Buddhist monk Shāntideva (685–763). One such quality includes helping others who are in need:

> May I be a guard for those who are protec-
> torless,
> A guide for those who journey on the road.
> For those who wish to go across the water,
> May I be a boat, a raft, a bridge.[13]

Another quality involves healing all beings from illness:

> For all those ailing in the world,
> Until their every sickness has been healed,
> May I myself become for them
> The doctor, nurse, the medicine itself.[14]

Bodhisattva qualities are also described in *The Thirty-seven Verses on the Practice of a Bodhisattva*, composed in the fourteenth century by the great Tibetan sage Gyalse Ngulchu Thogme (1297–1371). The vow of the bodhisattva is to liberate all beings from *saṃsāra*, the world of suffering.

---

[12] Karl Brunnhölzl, *Gone Beyond: The Prajñāpāramitā Sūtras, The Ornament of Clear Realization, and Its Commentaries in the Tibetan Kagyü Tradition,* vol. 1, trans. Karl Brunnhölzl (Ithaca, NY: Snow Lion Publications, 2010), 237.

[13] Shāntideva, *The Way of the Bodhisattva: A Translation of the Bodhicharyāvatāra,* rev. ed., trans. Padmakara Translation Group (Boston: Shambhala, 2006), 49 (chapter 3, verse 18).

[14] Ibid., 48 (chapter 3, verse 8).

> Now that I have this great ship, a precious
>   human life, so hard to obtain,
> I must carry myself and others across the
>   ocean of samsara.
> To that end, to listen, reflect, and meditate
> Day and night, without distraction, is the
>   practice of a bodhisattva.[15]

The goal of Buddhism is the ultimate benefit both of oneself and of others. Advanced bodhisattvas who have already realized profound wisdom and peace for themselves strive to put the happiness of others first. Gyalse Ngulchu Thogme writes from this advanced perspective:

> All suffering without exception arises from
>   desiring happiness for oneself,
> While perfect buddhahood is born from the
>   thought of benefiting others.
> Therefore, to really exchange
> My own happiness for the suffering of others
>   is the practice of a bodhisattva.[16]

Bodhisattvas are not merely compassionate ones who liberate all beings from the suffering of *saṃsāra*; they are also insightful beings who can inspire wisdom in others and apply wisdom to every situation. This simultaneous development of wisdom and compassion is described in the penultimate verse of *The Thirty-seven Verses on the Practice of a Bodhisattva*:

> In short, wherever I am, whatever I do,
> To be continually mindful and alert,
> Asking, "What is the state of my mind?"

---

[15] Dilgo Khyentse, *The Heart of Compassion,* 27–28 (verse 1).
[16] Ibid., 30 (verse 11).

> And accomplishing the good of others is the
> practice of a bodhisattva.[17]

Thich Nhat Hanh (b. 1926), a Vietnamese Zen Buddhist monk, teacher, and peace activist, insightfully notes that the water we experience in daily life is itself a bodhisattva: "Water is a good friend, a bodhisattva, which nourishes the many thousands of species on earth. Its benefits are numberless."[18] By viewing water as a bodhisattva, Nhat Hanh conveys that compassion and wisdom are directly present in this sacred source of life. Water is of great service to all beings, as life is completely dependent upon water for sustenance.

If we could learn to see water as a bodhisattva, this could significantly improve human-water relations. Regarding water as a bodhisattva would inspire us to relate to water as a teacher of compassion and wisdom and to treat water with love and respect. We would do our best not to take water for granted or treat it as a mere resource to be exploited for human gain. We would recognize that by polluting water, we would in effect be obscuring the ability for awakening for ourselves and for others. Seeing water as a bodhisattva would encourage the protection and restoration of waterways. This view would help us recognize that water is our teacher and that it can help us to wake up from self-centeredness and apathy and become of maximum service to others, including water and all beings dependent upon water.

The *Bodhicharyāvatāra* teaches that one of the aims of the bodhisattva is to help those who are thirsty by providing pure water to drink.

---

[17] Ibid., 36 (verse 36).

[18] Thich Nhat Hanh, "Look Deep and Smile: Thoughts and Experiences of a Vietnamese Monk: Talks and Writings of Thich Nhat Hanh," ed. Martine Batchelor, in *Buddhism and Ecology,* ed. Martine Batchelor and Kerry Brown (London: Cassell Publishers Limited, 1992), 105–6.

And may the naked now be clothed,
And all the hungry eat their fill.
And may those parched with thirst receive
Pure waters and delicious drink.[19]

Water, as a bodhisattva, provides its nourishing flow for the benefit of living beings. Water gives itself freely.

Water plays an important role in the mythology of bodhisattvas. As historian of Buddhism Malcolm David Eckel has observed, the eyes of bodhisattvas are "moist with compassion," which symbolizes "cognitive sophistication and emotional sensitivity."[20] Indeed, the bodhisattva Tārā, one of the most important deities in Himalayan Buddhism, was said in one origin myth to be born from the compassionate tears of the bodhisattva Avalokiteśvara.[21] Thus, the green form of Tārā, Śyāmatārā (who helps to deliver others from fear and is often depicted with her right leg extended, ready to help those in need) and the white form of Tārā, Sitatārā (who grants long life and is depicted with eyes on her hands, feet, and forehead so that she can see suffering everywhere) have watery tears of compassion as their point of origin and are embodiments of compassionate tears.

Water also is connected with Kuan-yin/Kannon, a famous female bodhisattva in East Asian Buddhism, who is often depicted holding a vase containing waters of purification, "seated on a rock gazing out across the water, or standing

---

[19] Shāntideva, *Way of the Bodhisattva,* 166 (chapter 10, verse 19).

[20] Malcolm David Eckel, "Hsüan-tsang's Encounter with the Buddha: A Cloud of Philosophy," in *Holy Tears: Weeping in the Religious Imagination,* ed. Kimberley Christine Patton and John Stratton Hawley (Princeton, NJ: Princeton University Press, 2005), 112.

[21] Martin Willson, *In Praise of Tara: Songs to the Saviouress* (Boston: Wisdom Publications, 1986), 123.

upon a floating lotus petal."[22] In China, she is a goddess of fisherman, and her shrines are often placed near water.[23] Furthermore, "rocks, willows, lotus pools or running water are often indications of her presence," and in "the prattle and tinkle of streams, her voice is heard."[24] Here we find more evidence that water is considered to be a bodhisattva.

THE SEVENTEENTH KARMAPA, THE BODHISATTVA, AND WATER

The compassionate wisdom of the bodhisattva is exemplified in the work of the Seventeenth Gyalwang Karmapa Ogyen Trinley Dorje (b. 1985), the Buddhist leader born in the Lhatok region of eastern Tibet. The Karmapa, head of the Karma Kagyu school of Tibetan Buddhism, is a promising young leader of environmental conservation who has done much to raise environmental awareness in the hearts and minds of his followers. *Gyalwa Karmapa* means "the Victorious One of Enlightened Activity."[25] The Karmapa is recognized by many Tibetan religious authorities, including the 14th Dalai Lama Tenzin Gyatso, to be the reincarnation of Dusum Khyenpa (1110–93), who founded the Karma Kagyu lineage and has continuously manifested through reincarnation into the present day.[26] In this section, I give a brief description of the Karmapa's environmental activities and his teachings on water. The Karmapa specifically draws on inspiration from the concept of the bodhisattva in his engaged

---

[22] John Blofeld, *Bodhisattva of Compassion: The Mystical Tradition of Kuan Yin* (Boston, MA: Shambhala Publications, Inc., 1978), 18.

[23] Ibid.

[24] Ibid., 66.

[25] Michele Martin, *Music in the Sky: The Life, Art and Teachings of the Seventeenth Karmapa Ogyen Trinley Dorje* (Ithaca, NY: Snow Lion Publications, 2003), 11.

[26] Buswell and Lopez, *The Princeton Dictionary of Buddhism,* 421–22.

work of training Buddhist monks and nuns to have ecological consciousness.

The Karmapa was born in rural eastern Tibet and was raised to see the natural world as sacred and deserving of love and care. As he recounts:

> I was born in the Tibetan wilderness, which means that I was fortunate enough to witness the natural or even pristine—to use your words—environment before it was subject to any significant modernization. I was brought up to experience the natural environment as fundamentally sacred and therefore the conservation of it as of tremendous importance. That instilled in me a very good habit, a habit of looking at the environment in a healthy way. And so as a result of that I have a particularly strong—I would say, heartfelt—love for nature, for the natural environment. My views on the need for environmental stewardship do not come from artificial or theoretical knowledge but from early experience.[27]

In an essay published in *Conservation Biology*, the Karmapa shares an early childhood experience that has helped to inform and motivate his environmental efforts throughout his life. He explains that during his childhood, there was an intense drought where he lived, and a local spring was drying up. The community knew that the very young Apo Gaga (Happy Brother), as he was called before he was recognized as the Karmapa when he was seven years old,[28] was an extraordinary child, and they asked him to plant a sapling at the source of the spring. As he recalls, "I remember leading prayers with the aspiration that this tree would help provide

---

[27] In Roger Cohn, "For Buddhist Leader, Religion and the Environment Are One," *Environment Yale 360* (April 16, 2015).

[28] Kagyu Office, "Karmapa," http://kagyuoffice.org/karmapa/.

water for all living beings nearby. Although I had no idea that what I was doing was an 'environmental' act, or what *watershed* meant, my love for nature and dedication to protect the environment sprouted from this seed."[29]

The Karmapa summarizes his vision as follows: "Protect the earth. Live simply. Act with compassion. Our future depends on it."[30] This simple statement, arising from within a Buddhist worldview that values compassion and wisdom, has profound implications for environmental awareness. A flourishing, resilient future for humans and the Earth community can be built by protecting the natural world from destruction, countering greed and living simply with minimal possessions, and acting with the compassionate intention to alleviate the suffering of others.[31]

Arising from his motivation to protect Earth, the Karmapa has helped to organize five different conferences from 2009 to 2013 to educate Buddhist monks and nuns about environmental conservation.[32] This conference series—Khoryug Conference on Environmental Protection for Tibetan Buddhist Monasteries and Nunneries in the Himalayas—has been very influential for spreading environmental awareness throughout Buddhist monastic communities and the local villages surrounding them.

During the second Khoryug conference, in October 2009, the Karmapa founded the Buddhist environmental network

---

[29] His Holiness the Seventeenth Gyalwang Karmapa Ogyen Trinley Dorje, "Walking the Path of Environmental Buddhism through Compassion and Emptiness," *Conservation Biology* 25, no. 6 (2011): 1094.

[30] Khoryug, "Activity," http://www.khoryug.com/karmapa-goals/.

[31] Stephanie Kaza, ed., *Hooked! Buddhist Writings on Greed, Desire, and the Urge to Consume* (Boston: Shambhala, 2005).

[32] These conferences were held in Sarnath (March 21–25, 2009), the Gyuto Monastery in Dharamsala (October 3–5, 2009), Bylakuppe, Mysore (November 14–16, 2010), Norbulingka Institute in Dharamsala (June 5–9, 2012), and the India International Centre in New Delhi (November 8–12, 2013).

Rangjung Khoryug Sungkyob Tsokpa (Association for the Protection of the Natural Environment), known simply as Khoryug.[33] This engaged project is based on Buddhist values of compassion and the wisdom of interdependence:

> Khoryug is a network of Buddhist monasteries and centers in the Himalayas working together on environmental protection of the Himalayan region with the aim of practically applying the values of compassion and interdependence towards the Earth and all living beings that dwell here. As Buddhist practitioners, we believe that our actions must flow from our aspiration to benefit all sentient beings and safeguard our mother Earth and that this positive change in our societies must begin with ourselves first. Khoryug aims to develop a partnership with community based organizations and NGOs wherever there is a member monastery or center so that together with our communities, we can help and protect all life on Earth now and for the future.[34]

On June 5, 2010, the Tesi Environmental Awareness Movement (TEAM), a nonprofit environmental organization based in Dharamsala that aims to "revive the ecological consciousness of the Tibetan people," gave Khoryug the Tesi Environmental Service Award.

Khoryug functions in close partnership with the nonprofit environmental conservation group World Wildlife Fund (WWF). Dekila Chungyalpa, the co-organizer and co-

---

[33] *Khoryug* is the word generally used for "environment" in the Tibetan language. It can also mean "surrounding area," "circumference," "horizon," and the outermost limit of the world in traditional Buddhist cosmology. The Tibetan and Himalayan Library, s.v. *khor yug,* http://www.thlib.org/reference/dictionaries/tibetan-dictionary/translate.php.

[34] Khoryug, "Vision," http://www.khoryug.com/vision/.

facilitator of the Khoryug conferences, is the founder of the WWF's Sacred Earth Program, which works with religious communities around the world to create faith-based environmental programs on "forestation and watershed restoration, river protection and clean up, climate change adaptation and mitigation, and combating illegal wildlife trade."[35] Through the Khoryug conferences, Chungyalpa has assisted the Karmapa in training representatives from fifty-five monasteries and nunneries in a number of environmental projects, including the following: "cleaning water sources, planting trees, separating waste and recycling, composting, installing solar heaters, converting to low-energy bulbs, ending the use of plastic bags and bottles, and much more."[36]

At the fifth Khoryug conference, in 2013, which focused on conservation of freshwater resources in the Himalayas, the monastic representatives were instructed on how to harvest rainwater, recharge groundwater, and protect and restore local sources of water.[37] Tenzin Norbu, who directs environment and development in the Central Tibetan Administration in Dharamsala, India, spoke of these goals for the participants of the fifth Khoryug conference: "When they go back, they should respect the value of the water. Since most of these are from the Himalayan area which is connected to the Tibetan plateau, they should know the importance of the place where

---

[35] World Wildlife Fund, "Sacred Earth: Faiths for Conservation"; World Wildlife Fund, "Tibetan Monasteries at Work for the Environment." The WWF Sacred Earth program is now housed at Yale University under the name Sacred Earth Initiative. See also World Wildlife Fund, "Dekila Chungyalpa."

[36] Kagyu Office, "Gyalwang Karmapa Launches Official Website for Environmental Protection: Khoryug.com" (December 22, 2009). See also Forum on Religion and Ecology at Yale, "Pope Francis and the Environment: Yale Examines Historic Climate Encyclical," transcript from the Panel on the Papal Encyclical, Yale University, April 8, 2015.

[37] Anjana Pasricha, "Buddhist Monks in the Himalayas Learn Fresh Water Conservation," *VOA News* (November 8, 2013).

they came from, so that they can also create local awareness on how important it is to protect the Himalayan glaciers."[38] The Karmapa has noted that the effects of climate change on the Tibetan Plateau have been a motivating cause of developing the Khoryug network.[39]

This five-day conference on freshwater conservation was held at the India International Centre in New Delhi on November 8–12, 2013, and included field trips to a wastewater treatment facility and the Yamuna River. At the wastewater treatment facility at the Centre for Science and Environment (CSE) in South Delhi, participants were given demonstrations of the treatment of wastewater, as well as rainwater harvesting. The CSE affirmed plans to partner with some of the Khoryug-member monasteries to implement similar wastewater treatment and rainwater harvesting programs in their communities so that the monasteries could conserve more water and become more self-sufficient in their water usage.

The second field trip included an excursion to the Yamuna River. As I explained in the previous chapter, this sacred river of northern India is greatly polluted as it flows through New Delhi. The Karmapa brought the conference participants to this river so that they could witness the pollution of the river firsthand. Seeing the polluted Yamuna was an eye-opening experience for those present, including a twenty-seven-year-old monk named Thinlay, who is a member of the Benchen monastery in Nepal. "It was my first time seeing something like this and it was horrible," he said. "This is what a dead river looks like. My eyes were full of tears. I thought, 'how could this happen?'"[40] Thinlay shared that this personal encounter with the polluted Yamuna was a powerful reminder of the

---

[38] Ibid.

[39] Cohn, "For Buddhist Leader, Religion and the Environment Are One."

[40] In Sara Fogel, "A River's Powerful Lesson," World Wildlife Fund (blog).

importance of caring for water in his local community. "We [Benchen monks] are leaders in our communities. We have a deep responsibility to pass on the message of environmental awareness," Thinlay said. "We must share with others how to reuse water for multiple purposes, conserve water and why it's important keep water sources clean."[41]

During this trip to the Yamuna the Karmapa convened a special event with the conference participants, local residents, and Manoj Misra, the director of the Yamuna Jiye Abhiyaan organization, which is focused on the restoration of the Yamuna River. They gathered together on the banks of a particularly polluted segment of the river to perform a river-blessing ceremony through prayers for the health of the river and the living beings supported by it.

> Standing together on its banks with the gathered monks and nuns, the Gyalwang Karmapa led prayers for the wellbeing of all living beings dependent on the river— from its pure Himalayan source right down to where it flows into the great Ganges river.
>
> This act of blessing once more symbolized the Gyalwang Karmapa's joining of spiritual inspiration with environmental activism, and reflects his understanding that environmental protection begins with changing our attitudes towards the planet. The Gyalwang Karmapa's environmental activities also reflect his single intention to protect and benefit all living beings through both traditional and modern methods.[42]

Performing this blessing for the polluted river and for all those who depend upon the river for nourishment is an act

---

[41] Ibid.

[42] Kagyu Office, "Khoryug Conference: Gyalwang Karmapa Blesses the Yamuna River" (November 11, 2013).

that embodies an integral water ethic that cares for water and all beings connected with those waters. By cultivating an aspiration to love and care for the natural world, this change in attitude and perception can lead to a positive change in actions.

This water blessing was not the first one that the Karmapa has enacted. On December 8, 2010, at the opening celebration of the year-long Karmapa 900 ceremony that honored the birth of Dusum Khyenpa, the founder of the Karma Kagyu lineage, the Karmapa blessed a clean drinking water facility that he donated to the Bodh Gaya Temple Management Committee. The Karmapa had the idea for the clean drinking water facility in the prior year during the 2009 Kagyu Monlam (Prayer Festival), when he noticed that many people were drinking bottled water and thus were generating a large amount of plastic waste. When he inquired about this, the Karmapa learned that public water facilities were not very numerous in Bodh Gaya, and people did not have access to clean drinking water. This is why he decided to give the water facility, which provides 500 liters (132 gallons) of clean drinking water per hour, to the temple.[43]

At this opening celebration the Karmapa performed prayers of auspiciousness and blessing for the water. This blessing was understood by the Buddhists who were in attendance to have transformed the ordinary tap water into blessed water, which the Tibetans see as *dudtsi*, sacred nectar of immortality.[44] In this instance, the Karmapa not only provided for the physical thirst of those who come to Bodh Gaya for pilgrimage, but also gave them sacred, blessed water that purifies their minds.

---

[43] Kagyu Office, "Gyalwang Karmapa Offers Clean Water to the People of Bodh Gaya as a Gift of Gratitude" (December 8, 2010).

[44] Ibid. See also Buswell and Lopez, *Princeton Dictionary of Buddhism*, 37.

During the celebration the Karmapa urged the protection of water:

> *Bodh Gaya is the place where Buddha was enlightened, which means that it is the birthplace of the most-valued teachings of wisdom and compassion. We should treat this land with respect and protect its natural environment. During Buddha's time, the river Niranjana flowed gloriously. But, these days, we hear that it is drying up. We must do everything we can to protect these water sources and to minimize wastes that are polluting this sacred land.*[45]

The Niranjana River (which is known today as the Lilajan River) holds a special place in the Buddhist tradition, as Siddhartha Gautama bathed in this river before he sat under a sacred fig tree in Bodh Gaya and attained enlightenment.[46] By drawing attention to this local river that has religious significance for Buddhists, the Karmapa is connecting religious values with environmental action.

The Karmapa has made clear that he has a strong desire to benefit the waters of Tibet and the Himalayas and to make sure that his work has long-term, practical consequences: "Whatever I do, I want it to have a long term impact and for it to be practical. If I have the opportunity, I want to create long term change and improvement of the environment in Tibet and Himalayas, especially to benefit the forests, the water and wildlife of this region."[47] The Tibetan Plateau contains the headwaters for many of Asia's rivers: Indus, Ganges, Yarlung Tsangpo (which becomes the Brahmaputra

---

[45] Kagyu Office, "Karmapa Offers Clean Water."

[46] Sanjeevkumar Tandle, *India History (Ancient Period)* (Solapur, Maharashtra, India: Laxmi Book Publication, 2014), 80

[47] Khoryug, "History," http://www.khoryug.com/karmapa-activity/.

downstream), Yangtze (Chang Jiang), Huang He (Yellow), Mekong, and Salween.[48] Tibet supplies drinking water to many Asian countries, including China, India, Bangladesh, Vietnam, Cambodia, Thailand, Laos, and Burma.[49] This region is considered to be the "Water Tower" of Asia and the "Land of Snows." It is estimated that the Tibetan Plateau contains "the water sources for about 40% of the world's population."[50] It is often called the "Roof of the World" due to its high altitude (the average elevation is 14,764 feet). It is also referred to as the "Third Pole," as this land contains the third largest amount of ice and water in the world after the Arctic and Antarctic. As the Karmapa warns, "If its water sources dry up or become contaminated, there will be fateful consequences for over a billion people. Because glacier melt is increasing as temperatures increase, both floods and water shortages will increase in the near future." The Karmapa goes on to say, "I invite all scholars and practitioners to help protect the Tibetan Plateau, which provides the water for much of mainland Asia. . . . As the Third Pole, Tibet is highly vulnerable to climate change and what happens there matters greatly to the rest of mainland Asia."[51]

The Karmapa embodies bodhisattva qualities. He is regarded as the emanation of the bodhisattva Avalokiteśvara, or Chenrezik in Tibetan. As the Tibetan translator Michele Martin explains: "Like the Dalai Lama, the Karmapa is regarded

---

[48] United Nations, *Sustainable Agriculture and Food Security in Asia and the Pacific* (Bangkok: United Nations Economic and Social Commission for Asia and the Pacific, 2009), 70.

[49] Keith Schneider and C. T. Pope, "China, Tibet, and the Strategic Power of Water," Circle of Blue website (May 8, 2008).

[50] Xiang Huanga, Mika Sillanpää, Egil T. Gjessing, and Rolf D. Vogt, "Water Quality in the Tibetan Plateau: Major Ions and Trace Elements in the Headwaters of Four Major Asian Rivers," abstract, *Science of the Total Environment* 407, no. 24 (2009): 6242–54.

[51] Ogyen Trinley Dorje, "Walking the Path of Environmental Buddhism through Compassion and Emptiness," 1095–96.

as an embodiment of compassion, represented by the deity
Chenrezik. The sole purpose of the Karmapa's incarnation
is to lead living beings from the suffering of samsara into
freedom—the realization of mind's deepest, pure nature."[52]
Avalokiteśvara, a figure appearing throughout Mahāyāna
scriptures, has many names evocative of the saving activity
of the bodhisattva. The Sanskrit name Avalokiteśvara is composed of *avalokita* (observing) and *iśvara* (lord), meaning one
who "observes the world and responds to the cries of living
beings."[53] The Tibetan Chenrezik follows this meaning: "one
who sees with penetrating vision."[54] East Asian versions, such
as the Chinese Kuan-yin or Kuan-shih-yin, and the Japanese
Kannon or Kanzeon, can be translated as "Regarder of the
World's Cries or Sounds."[55] Other evocative epithets from
the Tibetan include "Greatly Compassionate Transformer of
Beings" and "He Who Dredges the Depths of Samsara."[56]

The Karmapa teaches that Shāntideva, the author of the
Bodhicharyāvatāra (The Way of the Bodhisattva), is a model
for ecology. In "Walking the Path of Environmental Buddhism through Compassion and Emptiness," the Karmapa
writes this powerful statement: "If there were such a role
as a Buddhist saint of ecology, I would nominate the great
Indian scholar Shantideva."[57] Shāntideva, who saw the interdependence of all things, vowed to extinguish the suffering

---

[52] Martin, *Music in the Sky,* 11.

[53] Richard H. Robinson and Willard L. Johnson, *The Buddhist Religion: A Historical Introduction,* 4th ed. (Belmont, CA: Wadsworth Publishing Company, 1997), 108.

[54] I thank Aaron Weiss for his translation of Chenrezik. Personal communication, December 11, 2016.

[55] Taigen Dan Leighton, *Faces of Compassion: Classic Bodhisattva Archetypes and Their Modern Expression,* rev. ed. (Boston: Wisdom Publications, 2003), 184.

[56] Dilgo Khyentse, *The Heart of Compassion,* 50, 239n33.

[57] Ogyen Trinley Dorje, "Walking the Path of Environmental Buddhism through Compassion and Emptiness," 1095.

of others and provided a helpful guide for how to do this in his *Bodhicharyāvatāra*. As the Karmapa explains:

> The *Bodhicharyavatara* lays out the path to Buddha-hood through the cultivation of compassion and the insight into emptiness in the form of enlightened verses and gives inspiration to all who wish to renounce their own desires and ambitions in order to benefit all living beings.
>
> As the 17th Karmapa, I am confident that such Buddha activity can be directly translated into environmental protection. With this vision, we now have over 40 Kagyu monasteries and nunneries across the Himalayas implementing environmental projects to address issues such as forest degradation, water shortages, wildlife trade, climate change, and pollution, with guidance provided by nongovernmental organizations, including the World Wildlife Fund. We know that this is but a small drop in the ocean and the challenges we face are more complex and extensive than we can tackle alone. However, if each one of us were to contribute a single drop of clean water toward protecting the environment, imagine how pure this vast ocean could eventually be.[58]

As the Karmapa notes, no one person can solve the global environmental crisis. However, by working together, we have the potential to create enormous change, to build a flourishing future for our Earth community. The Karmapa's use of water imagery here is very helpful. It shows that every drop of water counts. Every clean drop of water contributes to a healthy ocean, while every polluted drop of water has harmful consequences for the ocean. Our actions are like drops of

---

[58] Ibid., 1097.

water—they can be pure or polluted. With every act we have the opportunity to benefit others or harm others.

The Karmapa has made numerous comments in which he draws connections between environmentalism and Buddhism. For example, at the end of the fifth Khoryug conference in 2013, the Karmapa said these powerful words: "The conservation of our environment—which is the ground of the existence of billions and billions of beings—must be our primary concern as Mahayana practitioners. Environmental conservation must be the very essence of our spiritual practice."[59]

The Karmapa links environmentalism with the two wings of the *dharma* (compassion for all beings and the understanding that all things are empty of inherent existence but instead interdependently exist): "The essence of Buddhism lies in the union of compassion and emptiness: the deeply felt dedication to alleviate the suffering of all living beings and the understanding that everything is devoid of self-nature. These two halves of a philosophical whole speak particularly to the goals of the environmental movement."[60]

The Karmapa goes on to say that "generating compassion for all living beings and turning that motivation into action is the most ecologically aware thing we can do."[61] The bodhisattva ethic is, at its core, an environmental ethic. Furthermore, the Karmapa says that for Buddhists the protection of the environment should arise from the bodhisattva vow. He opened the fourth Khoryug conference in 2012 with these words:

We should all try our hardest to protect the Tibetan Plateau and the Himalayas and preserve these ecosystems.

---

[59] Kagyu Office, "'Environmental Conservation Must Be the Essence of Our Spiritual Practice': Gyalwang Karmapa," November 12, 2014.

[60] Ogyen Trinley Dorje, "Walking the Path of Environmental Buddhism through Compassion and Emptiness," 1094.

[61] Ibid., 1095.

Preserving the biodiversity and the ecosystems of our region should be like the effortless practice of dharma for us. Our basic motivation to protect the environment should come from the pure desire to benefit all sentient beings on earth.[62]

In his interview with Yale Environment 360, he says that "the environmental emergency that we face is not just a scientific issue, nor is it just a political issue, it is also a moral issue."[63] He elaborates this point in "Walking the Path of Environmental Buddhism through Compassion and Emptiness":

For society to successfully address the environmental challenges of the 21st century, we have to connect these challenges to the individual choices people face on a daily basis. We cannot simply address the political and scientific aspects of problems such as climate change, intensive extraction of natural resources, deforestation, and wildlife trade. We must also address the social and cultural aspects of these problems by awakening human values and creating a movement for compassion, so that our very motivation in becoming environmentalists is to benefit other living beings.[64]

These words illustrate an integral approach to ecology. Here the Karmapa is implying that objectivist perspectives on ecological issues are incomplete until accompanied by psychospiritual and intersubjective responses.

---

[62] "World Environment Day and 4th Environmental Conference," *Tibet Post International* (June 7, 2012).

[63] In Cohn, "For Buddhist Leader, Religion and the Environment Are One."

[64] Ogyen Trinley Dorje, "Walking the Path of Environmental Buddhism through Compassion and Emptiness," 1096.

THE ECOSATTVA AND THE AQUASATTVA

The term *ecosattva* has been coined to signify bodhisattvas who are engaged with environmental activism. As Buddhism and ecology scholar Stephanie Kaza notes, "An 'ecosattva' is one form of a bodhisattva—someone who cares deeply about all beings and the health of the planet and is willing to take action after action to help all beings thrive."[65] This term was first coined in the 1990s as the name of a group of Zen practitioners at Green Gulch Farm in Sausalito, California, who drew inspiration from the Buddhist principle of compassion in their nonviolent protests of the logging of ancient redwoods in Northern California.[66]

The idea of the ecosattva is still being utilized today. In September 2015, the Buddhist organization One Earth Sangha launched an online "EcoSattva Training" course to help participants cultivate the "capacity to effectively engage on climate change and other ecological challenges, both thematically and locally, with courage, compassion and wisdom."[67] At the end of the training session, participants are invited to commit to "EcoSattva Vows" to work toward the "health, vitality and ease for all beings, seen and unseen, near and far, born and yet-to-be-born."[68] Participants are encouraged to repeat these vows daily to strengthen their intention to be of service to the world.

The suffering caused by local and global water crises calls for compassionate responses. An integral water ethic

---

[65] Stephanie Kaza, *Mindfully Green: A Personal and Spiritual Guide to Whole Earth Thinking* (Boston: Shambhala Publications, 2008), 13.

[66] Stephanie Kaza, "To Save All Beings: Buddhist Environmental Activism," in *Engaged Buddhism in the West,* ed. Christopher S. Queen (Somerville, MA: Wisdom Publications, 2000), 159, 170, 172.

[67] "EcoSattva Training," *One Earth Sangha,* online.

[68] "EcoSattva Vows," *One Earth Sangha,* online.

can draw much inspiration from Buddhist values of wisdom and compassion—the wisdom that all beings in the Earth community exist interdependently and the compassion for all suffering beings that arises from this wisdom. The bodhisattva archetype is a helpful guide for embodying such wisdom and compassion. The Karmapa is a living example of a person who has dedicated his life to this mission. His work raising ecological consciousness among Buddhist monks, nuns, and his many lay followers throughout the world (in specific connection to water issues in the Himalayas) is a helpful example of one who integrates Buddhism and ecology in a responsible way. Through the example of the bodhisattva and the Karmapa, an integral water ethic finds inspiration for engaging with water with compassionate wisdom.

As Thich Nhat Hanh says, water is a bodhisattva who nourishes all beings. Recognizing water as a bodhisattva involves recognizing the compassion and wisdom inherent in this sacred element of life. Water can be of great service to all beings if it is allowed to be itself. By recognizing that water is an active participant in communion with all life, people who have lost spiritual contact with water can learn to have a deeper sense of respect and care for this vital member of our Earth community. Cultivating intimacy with water can thus assist in cultivating intimacy with all our relations.

The bodhisattva archetype lends inspiration not only to the concept of the ecosattva, but also to a figure I call the *aquasattva*. The aquasattva is a bodhisattva who is deeply concerned for the well-being of water in all its different manifestations (e.g., waterways such as oceans, creeks, and rivers, but also bodies of water in the form of humans, animals, and plants). The aquasattva sees water as a bodhisattva, a wise and compassionate teacher who helps awaken wisdom and compassion within the practitioner. Cultivating compassion for water and experiencing water as an embodiment of compassion are practices through which we can contribute to a flourishing future for our Earth community. By restoring the health of water, by working for water justice for all, by practicing an integral water ethic, we are able to help water realize its potential to be of service to all beings.

The aquasattva is one who says: I vow to liberate water and all beings from suffering. When I am of service to water, I help water become of service to all beings. My own awakening is the awakening of water. By awakening my potential to become an aquasattva in human form, I help water awaken to its own aquasattva potential. May I, like water, flow freely for the benefit of all beings.

5

Contemplative Practices
for Cultivating
an Integral Water Ethic

As I argue throughout this book, this is a crucial moment in history when humans must reinvent their relationship to water and develop an integral water ethic. This chapter focuses on a variety of contemplative practices that can assist in the cultivation of an integral water ethic.

According to a report published by the Center for Contemplative Mind in Society, a contemplative practice can be defined as "a practice undertaken with the intention to quiet the mind and to cultivate a personal capacity for deep concentration, presence, and awareness. Ideally, the insights that arise from the mind, body, and heart in this contemplative state can be applied to one's everyday life." There are many different forms of contemplative practices, including "single-minded concentration, such as meditation, mindful movement (i.e., Hatha Yoga, T'ai Chi, walking meditation), contemplative prayer, reading of sacred texts (i.e., Lectio Divina), focused experiences in nature, contemplative physical or artistic practices (i.e., Buddhist sand mandalas), and

certain forms of social activism in a context of mindfulness."
In addition, contemplative practices include "rituals and cer-
emonies designed to create sacred space and to mark rites of
passage and the cyclical nature of time," as well as "engaged
interpersonal dialogue." As a whole, contemplative practices
have the ability "to bring different aspects of oneself into focus, to help develop personal goodness and compassion, and
to awaken an awareness of the interconnectedness of all life."
For a helpful diagram of different examples of contemplative
practices, see the "Tree of Contemplative Practices."[1]

In what follows I share six contemplative practices that can
help facilitate deeper intimacy with water and a greater sense
of care for water. Two meditations (the Water *Kasina* and the
Bowl of Tears) were developed by others, while the other
four practices are ones I have developed. These practices
are inspired by taiji walking meditation, as well as Buddhist
meditation and compassion practices. Many of these practices
share the theme of mindfulness. Mindfulness (*smṛti*) is "com-
monly used in meditative contexts to refer to the ability to
remain focused on a chosen object without forgetfulness or
distraction."[2] Thich Nhat Hanh explains it using the example
of drinking water: "When you drink a glass of water and are
aware that you are drinking a glass of water, that is mindfulness of drinking water."[3]

One commonality among these practices is that they focus
on how water is an elemental link that connects the self and
the world. By experiencing the human body as a body of
water, we can find our place in the watery world and learn to

---

[1] Maia Duerr, *A Powerful Silence: The Role of Meditation and Other
Contemplative Practices in American Life and Work* (Northampton, MA:
The Center for Contemplative Mind in Society, 2004), 37–39.

[2] Robert E. Buswell, Jr., and Donald S. Lopez, Jr., *The Princeton Dictionary of Buddhism* (Princeton, NJ: Princeton University Press, 2014), 831.

[3] Thich Nhat Hanh, *Teachings on Love* (Berkeley, CA: Parallax Press,
1998), 42.

extend our sense of care to all bodies of water. Practices are important for gaining a more vivid sense of the connection between self and world, between humans and water, between an individual and all beings.

Embodied, experiential practices can help us to have a more integral understanding of the fundamental importance of water for life, as well as the difficult facts about the global water crisis. As the philosopher Mark Johnson explains, "understanding is profoundly embodied"; it is not a mere "abstract intellectual grasping of concepts and their relations" but instead "is a full-bodied, full-blooded, fully passionate process that reaches down into the visceral depths of our incarnate experience and connects us functionally to our physical-cultural world."[4] Because understanding is always already embodied, it is important to listen and pay attention to our bodies and not neglect them in favor of abstract cognition. Practices provide an experiential ground from which we can relate to water in a more loving and compassionate way. Engaging in practices for cultivating a more intimate relationship with water will help us to engage water issues from a place of greater empathy and compassion.

How can we learn to see water in a new way? How can we learn to have a more caring and respectful relationship with water? It takes practice. Through the repetition of practice, we can cultivate new habits that are more in tune with our intentions. Contemplative practices, as the Mind and Life Education Research Network reports, "are structured and socially scaffolded activities that train skills by placing some constraint or imposing some discipline on a normally unregulated mental or physical habit." Furthermore, "at the heart of such practices is repetition and practice to cultivate

---

[4] Mark Johnson, "Embodied Understanding," *Frontiers in Psychology* 6 (June 29, 2015): 875.

more positive habits of mind."[5] Because they can lead to the cultivation of positive habits, contemplative practices are a crucial component of an integral water ethic. Feeling into the flows of water, seeing the beauty of water, tasting this refreshing drink, hearing the sound of immense waterfalls or meandering creeks, smelling rain on the earth—these simple activities have the ability to be meaningful and powerful. Through directly engaging with water, we can heighten our ability to care for water and all our Earth community. Through interacting with water with all our senses, we can notice patterns and see meaningful connections.

Practices can help us shift from the dominant way of interacting with water as a mere resource, commodity, and sewer, and move toward an integral water ethic that cares for water as a sacred source of life. As Christopher Chapple, a professor at Loyola Marymount University who specializes in South Asian religions and ecology, explains:

> By engaging in a regular spiritual practice that includes acknowledgement of the elements, a greater sensitivity may be cultivated toward the natural world. Enhanced consciousness of water is essential in the process of environmental healing. Meditation practices on water, from any tradition, help bring one out of what Thomas Berry calls the technological trance. As our intimacy with water increases, our ability to be informed about and responsive to such issues as waste and privatization will be enhanced.[6]

---

[5] Richard J. Davidson et al., "Contemplative Practices and Mental Training: Prospects for American Education," *Child Development Perspectives* 6, no. 2 (2012): 147, 150.

[6] Christopher Key Chapple, "Jainism and Ecology: Transformation of Tradition," in The *Oxford Handbook of Religion and Ecology*, ed. Roger S. Gottlieb, 147–59 (New York: Oxford University Press, 2006), 157–58.

Spiritual practices connected with water can bring about greater sensitivity of and intimacy with the waters of the world, thus leading to more compassionate and engaged responses to water crises. Furthermore, contemplative practices help to foster greater resilience and adaptation to stress and change, which is highly valuable in light of the global water crisis.[7]

In what follows I share various practices to assist in the cultivation of an integral water ethic. These practices can be done with the instructions provided; however, it is generally helpful to have a teacher to assist throughout one's practice.[8] My intention in including the practices below is to share accessible, practical ways that can assist us in engaging with water with more respect and care.

DRINKING A GLASS OF WATER

We can begin with a very basic activity that we often do unconsciously many times throughout the day: drinking water. This practice asks us to pay close attention as we drink.

Fill up a glass with clean drinking water. Listen to the sounds the water is making as it fills the glass. What do you notice? Before taking a sip, take a moment and hold this glass in your hands. Look into the water. What do you see? Smell it. Does it have a smell? Dip your finger into the water. Is the water cool, warm, or the same temperature as your body? As you hold this glass of water, open your heart and allow yourself to speak to water. What would you like to say to water?

---

[7] Teresa I. Sivilli and Thaddeus W. W. Pace, "The Human Dimensions of Resilience: A Theory of Contemplative Practices and Resilience," The Garrison Institute (2014).

[8] I encourage you to seek out teachers if you have questions or need further guidance. Likewise, if you have any health constraints that may affect your ability to perform any of these practices, I strongly recommend that you check with a medical professional first.

You can offer prayers, intentions, gratitude, or anything else that comes up for you. Now, slowly bring the glass to your lips and take some water into your mouth. Hold it in your mouth for a moment before you swallow. Now, swallow this water. How does it feel to drink this clean water? What do you notice? Allow yourself to slowly drink this glass of water, paying attention to any feelings or thoughts that arise for you.

This practice of mindfully drinking water is inspired by a daily practice that I do before each writing session. Throughout the long and hard process of writing this book, I had a strong urge to create a daily water ritual, to ritualize my writing process, and to help give this book a larger sense of meaning. When thinking of different rituals that I could incorporate into my writing, I decided to work with a special water bowl. At the beginning of each writing session, I would fill the bowl with clean water, hold it close, and say a prayer, asking to hear water's voice. Then I would drink this water.

I have found that this ritual has greatly empowered my writing and has helped contextualize this book within a larger sacred container. Each time I perform the ritual in slightly different ways. I say various prayers, I ask different questions, I sing new songs—all with an intention to develop a more intimate relationship with water. I ask the water to let me know it, to open my ears so that I can hear its messages. I ask water to speak through me, so that I can share its stories with others. This practice helps me remember that water connects all life through its different manifestations throughout the hydrosphere.

One of the most profound parts of this ritual is the simple act of mindfulness. Before speaking, praying, or singing to water, I am silent. I hold the bowl of water and practice listening. While I am silent, I allow my body to resonate with water and tune in to water's energy. I am mindful that I am holding water and that I am about to drink water, that this water will move through me and become a vital part of my body. This simple act of holding the water bowl, standing in silence in front of my altar, gives me a feeling of peace. I find this ritual helpful in dissolving the anxiety that often builds up around the writing process.

The water bowl that I use for this daily ritual is itself very special to me. It is a small blue and green ceramic bowl that that was created for Thomas Berry's memorial service at the Cathedral of St. John the Divine on September 26, 2009. This bowl is part of a set of 108 bowls that form a water mala.[9] The water mala bowls were created by Hermitage Heart before the memorial service, and during the service they were arranged on blue and gold fabric in a pattern that looked like a fusion of meditation beads and a meandering river.[10] After the memorial service, the 108 bowls in this water mala were given to 108 friends, family members, and colleagues of Thomas Berry who were invited to attend to water as a "living being" that is "precious and sacred."

One of my first encounters with Thomas Berry was through a film titled *Thomas Berry: The Great Story.* I watched it in my very first class at the California Institute of Integral Studies, "World Religions and Ecology," with Mary Evelyn Tucker and John Grim. The segment of the film that most stands out in my mind is of Thomas Berry saying:

Last night the moon was shining on this wonderful bay. And I asked the moon, "What should I say?" And the moon said, "Tell them the story." And I asked the wind, "What should I say?" He said, "Tell them the story." And I asked the clover out on the lawn, "What should

---

[9] *Mala,* a Sanskrit word meaning "garland" or "rosary," refers to meditation beads ritually used by Hindus and Buddhists for mantra recitations. Buswell and Lopez, *Princeton Dictionary of Buddhism*, 520.

[10] For a video of the mala, see "108 Bowls: A Water Mala," YouTube.

I say?" And the clover said, "Tell them the story—my story, the mountain's story, the river's story, your story, the Indians' story, the Great Story."[11]

Watching the film was a powerful introduction to one of Berry's main ideas: every being in the world is asking to tell its story, which is one way of telling the story of the universe. With this book I am trying to tell the stories of water, to listen to water, to respect the agency of water. It feels especially powerful to be drinking daily from a water mala bowl created for Thomas Berry's memorial, writing a book that involves telling the stories of water.

Drinking water from this bowl in this way helps me remember one of Berry's key teachings: we humans are dwelling in a living universe, composed not of a collection of objects but of a communion of subjects.[12] We can learn to commune intimately with all beings in the universe, including water. Through various mindfulness practices, including this one with the water mala bowl, my relationship with water is being transformed. I am learning to experience water as a being with interiority. Recalling the discussion in Chapter 1, water's subjectivity is expressed through the self-organizing dynamics that manifest in the form of whirlpools, eddies, snowflakes, and waves.

This water ritual is helpful in many ways. One thing that is becoming clear through the ritual is that water is my witness, my accountability partner. I am pledging daily to have love and compassion, to be of service to water and all beings. I am speaking these intentions into water, sharing my deepest

---

[11] *Thomas Berry: The Great Story*, produced by Nancy Stetson and Penny Morell, 2002.

[12] Thomas Berry, *Evening Thoughts: Reflecting on Earth as Sacred Community*, ed. Mary Evelyn Tucker (San Francisco: Sierra Club Books and University of California Press, 2006), 17.

aspirations with water. Then I am drinking the water that is vibrant with my love and desire to be of service. As this water moves through my body, it is becoming me, integrating into my organic systems. As this water is becoming me, it is helping me become who I want to be: a humble and loving person who strives to be of service to all our relations. Water is transforming my life continuously. I owe so much to this wonderful friend, my aquatic companion, my witness, my teacher, and my guide. I want to give back with all my life. May I live and breathe in service of you, water, and in service of all beings.

If you would like to try this practice yourself or share it with others, I recommend that you simply be present with the water that you are about to drink. Then, when you drink water, be mindful that you are drinking water. See what connections come up for you. You can do this practice regularly throughout the day, each time you take a drink of water. In this way the simple and regular act of drinking water can be a way to return to mindfulness.

GRATITUDE WALK

Another practice that can engender a deeper relationship with water is the Gratitude Walk. To perform this practice, simply go on a walk in your neighborhood to visit your local creek, river, lake, or other body of water. If you live close to the ocean, take a walk along the beach. Or, if you are up for an olfactory adventure, go visit your local wastewater treatment plant. Any body of water will work for this exercise, whether it is a natural body of water or a constructed body of water.

As you walk, be mindful of everything you see, hear, touch, taste, and smell. Pay attention especially to all the different forms of water that you encounter. Allow your curiosity to guide you. Begin to greet the world around you. Your greeting does not have to be audible, though it can be if you would like. The main point is to acknowledge that you share a world with other living beings that have subjectivity. As you continue to walk, feel your heart opening with love for water and the Earth community. Give gratitude for all that you encounter. "Imagine for a moment that everything you see, hear, smell, touch, and taste is your very best friend."[13] As you spend time with water, feel as if you are spending time with someone who is very special and dear to you.

This practice is one way to begin to see water and all beings as having subjectivity. This is a way to be in dialogue with the Earth community, to gain a deeper sense of intimacy with the world around you. This practice can help you to see that everything in the world is alive, that matter is sacred, that life force (qi) pervades all things. By participating in this practice regularly, you can begin to see your relation with the world change. Instead of seeing the world as full of passive, inert, lifeless objects, you can begin to see the world as a communion of living subjects.

This practice arose out of an experience I had one evening in the fall of 2011 at the Esalen Institute in Big Sur, California. I was there for the annual conference-retreat of our Philosophy, Cosmology, and Consciousness program at the California Institute of Integral Studies. I found that as I walked through the beautiful land, I felt intense gratitude for every being that I encountered. As I made my way across the bridge over Hot Springs Creek, a creek that divides the Esalen property by flowing out of the canyon and into the ocean, I heard this question: *How can I be of service?* At first I thought this was my own personal question, coming from within. But

---

[13] Michael Carroll, *Fearless at Work: Timeless Teachings for Awakening Confidence, Resilience, and Creativity in the Face of Life's Demands* (Boston: Shambhala Publications, 2012), 173.

then I realized that this question was simultaneously coming from the creek, too. I was asking water how I could be of service at the same time that water itself was asking this question. I immediately felt the power of the question, the reciprocity of the one who is serving and the one who is being served. With that experience I began to consciously practice seeing water as a person. I began to pay closer attention to the voices of water. This experience has inspired me to listen to the messages that come up every time I cross a bridge. Crossing a bridge has become an experiment of being mindful of the personhood of water, an exercise to pay attention, to engage with the subjectivity of water.

Furthermore, the question *How can I be of service?* has a direct connection with the archetype of the bodhisattva. Hearing this question arise from within myself at the same time as I heard it arise from the creek was an experience of feeling the innate capacity of wisdom and compassion within myself as it is simultaneously present within water. Offering gratitude for water's existence and the innumerable gifts it provides to us and other living beings is a way to learn to dwell within a communion of subjects.

I encourage you to try this practice any time you are out on a walk. Offering gratitude to the beings with whom you come into contact is a way to change your relationship with the world. This simple practice can have profound results and can engender a deeper sense of intimacy and empathy with others.

THE WATER *KASIṆA*: OBSERVING THE WATER ELEMENT THROUGH MEDITATION

Another practice that can help engender an integral water ethic is the early Buddhist practice of observing the elements referred to as *kasiṇa*, a Pāli word that means "totality" or "universal" and signifies a "'visualization device' that serves as the meditative foundation for the 'totality' of the mind's attention to an object of concentration."[14] Christopher Chapple notes that this meditation, found in The Path of Purification *(Visuddhimagga),* a Buddhist text written by Bhadantácariya Buddhaghosa in the fifth century, is the earliest description of a water meditation that he could find in his research.[15] As Chapple describes, this is a practice that helps to cultivate an awareness of the five elements of earth, water, fire, air, and space by paying attention to how everything in the universe shares their bodily material. This practice "reminded the practitioner of the commonality of elements: all persons and all things are composed of these essential components."[16] For example, one way to observe the element of water involves gazing at a bowl of clear water, associating words related to water, and repeating these words until you see the elemental connection between the bowl of water and other forms of water throughout your body and the world.[17] You can engage in a meditation on the five elements for about twenty minutes twice a day for several months. In the first few weeks you are to focus on earth, then water, fire, air, and space (moving from the gross to the subtle).

Doing such a practice of observing the elements has the ability to expand our awareness of and sensitivity to the cos-

---

[14] Buswell and Lopez, *Princeton Dictionary of Buddhism*, 425.

[15] Christopher Key Chapple, "Water as Wellspring of Life: The Emerging Alliance of Religion and Ecology," presentation at the Parliament of World Religions, Barcelona, Spain, 2004, 2.

[16] Christopher Key Chapple, "India's Earth Consciousness," in *The Soul of Nature,* ed. Michael Tobias and Georgianne Cowan (New York: Continuum, 1994), 147.

[17] Chapple lists some of the Pāli words for water given in *The Path of Purification (Visuddhimagga):* "water *(āpo),* rain *(ambu),* liquid *(udaka),* dew *(vāri),* and fluid *(salila)*." Chapple, "India's Earth Consciousness," 148.

mos. By recognizing the reciprocity of the human and the world, we can learn how to cultivate "an intimacy with the elements."[18] Such an intimacy is described by Chapple as an environmental ethic coming from "sacred attention" to the body and the earth: "An environmental ethic emerges from a sacred attention *(puruṣa)* to the needs of one's body and the earth itself, both of which become manifest through the creative matrix *(parakṛti)*."[19] An integral water ethic can be cultivated through attention to the intimate elemental relationship between the human body and the cosmic world.

As noted above, this practice is to be done for twenty minutes twice a day for several months. The practice can be performed at any time of day or night, and to help with consistency I recommend practicing at the same time each day for each of the two sessions. For example, you could practice first thing in the morning and again right before you go to bed. The main point is to have a regular practice so that you can learn to cultivate an intimacy with the elements. The more that you perform this practice, the more you will be able to engage effortlessly in this practice in the parts of the day when you are not officially meditating. In that way, you will find that seeing bodies of water, engaging in conversations about water, or hearing the sounds of water will bring a felt sense of continuity of the water flowing throughout the world and throughout your body.

EMBODYING THE ELEMENTS WALKING MEDITATION

This next practice arises from within the Chinese tradition of taijiquan (tai chi chuan). This internal martial art can be

---

[18] Chapple, "Water as Wellspring of Life," 4.
[19] Chapple, "India's Earth Consciousness," 146.

translated as "great ultimate fist."[20] Taijiquan is a form of qigong (chi gong), which means "working with the life energy, learning how to control the flow and distribution of qi to improve the health and harmony of mind and body."[21] Qi (chi) is a complex word. "The original meaning of the Chinese word Qi was 'universal energy.' Every type of energy in the universe is called Qi."[22] Chi can be translated as "material force," "vital force," and "vital power," and "denotes the psychophysiological power associated with blood and breath."[23] The power of qi felt in the body is a manifestation of the qi flowing through the entire universe.

One of the key principles of taiji is to learn to move your body as if you are flowing like water. Many movements mimic the flowing nature of water. Sometimes students are asked to move as if they are swimming through the air, floating in a pool of water, or treading through thick, viscous molasses or honey.[24] These embodied imaginal exercises are meant to draw out the intimate intertwinement of self and world.

For seven years during my doctoral studies I led free weekly integral taiji and qigong classes at the California Institute of Integral Studies, as well as occasional workshops and private lessons. One of the exercises that I developed is

---

[20] *Tai* means "great" or "large"; *chi* is a superlative connoting that which is ultimate or supreme; and *chuan* refers to fist or boxing and sometimes connotes a technique of the martial arts. Bruce Frantzis, *The Big Book of Tai Chi: Build Health Fast in Slow Motion* (London: Thorsons, 2003), 3–5.

[21] Kenneth S. Cohen, *The Way of Qigong: The Art and Science of Chinese Energy Healing* (New York: Ballantine Books, 1997), 3.

[22] Shou-Yu Liang and Yang Jwing-Ming, *Hsing Yi Chuan: Theory and Applications: Analysis of Fighting Tactics and Spirit* (Jamaica Plain, MA: Yang's Martial Arts Association Publication Center, 1990), 4.

[23] Wing-Tsit Chan, *A Source Book in Chinese Philosophy*, trans. Wing-Tsit Chan (Princeton, NJ: Princeton University Press, 1963), 784.

[24] Cohen, *Way of Qigong*, 61; Man-ch'ing Cheng and Robert W. Smith, *T'ai-chi: The "Supreme Ultimate" Exercise for Health, Sport, and Self-Defense*, 2nd ed. (North Clarendon, VT: Tuttle Publishing, 2004), 10.

a taiji walking meditation called Embodying the Elements, which focuses on the elements of earth, water, fire, and air. By learning to embody these elements, the practitioner is able to become mindful of the intimate intertwining of the elements of the world and the elements that compose our human bodies.

The following practice can be performed by anyone, regardless of prior taiji experience. Having a qualified teacher is helpful but is not necessary for this particular practice, as the written instructions invite improvisational movement that is connected with imagination. This practice can be performed indoors or outside at any time of day. However, it is best not to practice immediately after eating a meal; instead, wait at least an hour or two so that the food can digest.

The practice begins in stillness. Spend a few moments focusing on your breath. Be calm and at peace. Then begin to slowly shift your weight from one side to the other. Now, begin to slowly walk. Be mindful of your body. Relax your mind.

As you are slowly walking, bring to consciousness the water element. Allow your body to flow like water in any way that you would like. Bring to mind some particular body of water, either a waterway that is very familiar to you or perhaps a new waterway that you have recently visited. As you hold this water in your mind, allow your body to imitate the flows of this water. How does this water move? Is it slowly meandering? Is it raging or churning? Feel the waters of your body connected to the waters of this place. Flow like water.

Now bring to consciousness the air element that is connected to this body of water. How does it feel to be the air flowing with this water? Is it cool or warm? Is the air moving softly or forcefully? Feel your breath connected with this air. Breathe in; breathe out. Feel your breath connected with life force, with the breath of all beings. Flow like air.

Next, bring to consciousness the fire element that is present at this place. Feel the heat of the sun warming the earth. See the rays of sunlight sparkling on the surface of the water. Feel the fires of your body connected with the fires of this place. Flow like fire.

Now bring to consciousness the earth element that is present at this place. With your body, trace the contours of the earth. Feel the solidity, the weight of earth here. Feel the solidity and weight of your body. Flow like earth.

Finally, bring to consciousness the place as a whole. Feel the watershed. Feel all the elements balanced, held together in a unique way. Notice how your own body is—a unique configuration of cosmic energy (qi) similar to the unique configuration of qi that is this watershed. Feel qi flowing within and as this place. Feel qi flowing within and as your body. Notice how your body is a miniature watershed. Water continually cycles within you, and it becomes you. You are an intimate part of the hydrological cycle. Your personal self mirrors cosmic energy. Your personal self is cosmic flow.

With this elemental walking meditation, we are embodying a particular place, a particular watershed. With our consciousness we are able to bring a distant place into this present moment. We embody this watershed in our consciousness, in our minds. Now embody this watershed in your conscience, in your heart. Feel into the emotions associated with this place. Why did this particular body of water call out to you in this practice? Is it spectacular, epic, beautiful? Is it a pristine place that brings you immense joy and wonder when you visit it? Is it a familiar place, a special home to you?

As you do this practice, send out intentions that all water may be flowing freely like this water is. Pray for all water to be this healthy and vibrant. Bringing to mind this body of water helps you renew your intention and commitment to be of service to water, to have love and compassion for water and all beings. May all water flow to the sea with joy and peace.

Neo-Confucian scholar Tu Weiming explains that we humans can embody the cosmos in our minds and hearts, in our consciousness and conscience:

> Human beings are thus an integral part of the "chain of being," encompassing Heaven, Earth, and the myriad things. However, the uniqueness of being human is the intrinsic capacity of the mind to "embody" *(t'i)* the cosmos in its conscience and consciousness. Through this embodying, the mind realizes its own sensitivity, manifests true humanity and assists in the cosmic transformation of Heaven and Earth.[25]

Through our ability to embody the cosmos, we are the universe knowing itself. As Thomas Berry writes:

> The human is that being in whom the universe reflects on and celebrates itself and its numinous origin in its own, unique mode of conscious self-awareness. All living beings do this in their own unique way, but in the human, this becomes a dominant mode of functioning. It is not that we think on the universe; the universe, rather, thinks *itself*, in us and through us.[26]

In our human bodies we can sense qi, the vital energy that flows throughout the universe. We can gain an intimacy with

---

[25] Tu Weiming, *Confucian Thought: Selfhood as Creative Transformation*, SUNY Series in Philosophy (Albany: State University of New York Press, 1985), 132.

[26] Thomas Berry with Thomas Clark, *Befriending the Earth: A Theology of Reconciliation between Humans and the Earth*, ed. Stephen Dunn, CP, and Anne Lonergan (Mystic, CT: Twenty-Third Publications, 1991), 21.

the cosmos through an intimacy with our human body. In this way we can gain a felt sense of how the boundaries of our human bodies blur with the world around us, as the same vital energy composes and flows through us all.

THE BOWL OF TEARS

Another practice that is useful in the context of an integral water ethic is the Bowl of Tears. This practice was created by the eco-philosopher and activist Joanna Macy as part of The Work that Reconnects, an empowerment process that helps to "restore our sense of connection with the web of life and with one another."[27] Designed as part of a series of practices for "Honoring Our Pain in the World," the Bowl of Tears goes as follows:

> Fill a clear glass bowl about one third full of water and place it in the center of the circle on the floor or a table. The water represents our tears for the world. All are invited to come to the bowl as they are moved. Dipping a hand in the water and letting it trickle through their fingers, they can say, "My tears are for . . . " and speak of specific beings and places.[28]

A facilitator can encourage participants to name what their tears are for, giving voice to their despair and pain. Once everyone has had the opportunity to pour water through their fingers, the group can sit in silence for a few moments. Then

---

[27] Joanna Macy and Chris Johnstone, *Active Hope: How to Face the Mess We're in without Going Crazy* (Novato, CA: New World Library, 2012), 6.

[28] Joanna Macy and Molly Brown, *Coming Back to Life: The Updated Guide to The Work that Reconnects* (Gabriola Island, British Columbia: New Society Publishers, 2014), 129.

the facilitator can lead the group as the participants slowly get up and walk outside together. The ritual concludes by mindfully pouring out the bowl of tears into a body of water outside (pond, lake, creek, river, or the ocean). The facilitator can remind the group that "the pain we feel for the world is no private pathology; it connects us with Earth and one another."[29]

This ritual helps us to get in touch with the pain that we feel for the world. This water ritual brings to light the intimate intertwining of self and world. When we cry, we are giving the waters of our bodies back to the world. We are allowing ourselves to acknowledge the permeability of our bodies, to feel the boundaries of our self open up and touch the world. Macy often reminds us that "our tears for the world are the tears of Gaia."[30]

In an interview Macy elaborates on the spiritual significance of feeling pain and letting your pain overflow through tears:

Feeling the pain of the world is not a weakness. This is God-given or, put another way, an aspect of our Buddha nature. This openness of heart that characterizes the caring individual is a function of maturity. Don't ever apologize for the tears you shed on behalf of other beings. This is, in its essence, not craziness, but compassion. This capacity to speak out on behalf of others, because you have the right to, because you can suffer with them, is part of our spiritual nature.[31]

Water wants to serve us, to nurture us with its life-giving powers. As Thich Nhat Hanh says: "Water is a good friend, a

---

[29] Ibid.

[30] Ibid.

[31] Mary NurrieStearns, "Transforming Despair: An Interview with Joanna Macy," http://www.personaltransformation.com/joanna_macy.html.

bodhisattva, which nourishes the many thousands of species on earth. Its benefits are numberless."[32] Bodhisattvas hear the cries of suffering of the world and are compassionately present with that suffering. Water as a bodhisattva hears the cries of thirst around the world and gives its waters freely to all without discrimination. Water teaches us how to serve others. When we can learn to be like water, to be the water bodies that we are, then we can learn how to serve water with the love and respect that are so urgently called for in this time in history.

Thich Nhat Hanh was once asked this question: "What do we most need to do to save our world?" He responded, "What we most need to do is to hear within us the sounds of the Earth crying."[33] When we listen to the cries of suffering of the world, we are able to open our hearts and cultivate compassion. As Macy reminds us: "The heart that breaks open can hold the whole universe. Your heart is that large. Trust it. Keep breathing."[34] The heart that is broken open with suffering for the world can share compassion and love with all beings.

The Bowl of Tears ritual can work for groups of any size. It is helpful to have a facilitator who can share basic instructions at the beginning and can lead the group outside at the closing of the ritual. Macy recommends doing this practice in a group format: "Group work is most effective because we are conditioned to think that despair is a personal problem that we must handle alone. A group experience restores a deep faith in life. There is a strong sense of coming home at last to one another, so that we face this together."[35] By sharing our suf-

---

[32] Thich Nhat Hanh, "Look Deep and Smile: Thoughts and Experiences of a Vietnamese Monk: Talks and Writings of Thich Nhat Hanh," ed. Martine Batchelor, in *Buddhism and Ecology*, ed. Martine Batchelor and Kerry Brown (New York: Cassell Publishers Limited, 1992), 105–6.

[33] In Joanna Macy, *World as Lover, World as Self: Courage for Global Justice and Ecological Renewal* (Berkeley, CA: Parallax Press, 2007), 94–95.

[34] Ibid., 129.

[35] Joanna Macy, in NurrieStearns, "Transforming Despair."

fering with others, we are able to find courage to undertake compassionate action together.

TONGLEN: CULTIVATING COMPASSION FOR POLLUTED WATERS

This practice is based on *tonglen*, a Tibetan word that means "giving and taking."[36] *Tonglen* is oriented around receiving the suffering of others and offering compassion in return. It is a method for cultivating *bodhicitta*, the intention to attain enlightenment "in order to liberate all sentient beings in the universe from suffering."[37] *Tonglen* is a profound method for cultivating compassion that involves meditating on the suffering that is present within us and throughout the world. As Tibetan nun and teacher Pema Chödrön explains:

> Tonglen practice is a method for connecting with suffering—our own and that which is all around us, everywhere we go. It is a method for overcoming our fear of suffering and for dissolving the tightness of our hearts. Primarily it is a method for awakening the compassion that is inherent in all of us, no matter how cruel or cold we might seem to be. . . .
>
> Tonglen reverses the usual logic of avoiding suffering and seeking pleasure. In the process, we become liberated from very ancient patterns of selfishness. We begin to feel love for both ourselves and others; we begin to take care of ourselves and others. Tonglen awakens our compassion and introduces us to a far bigger view of reality.[38]

---

[36] Buswell and Lopez, *Princeton Dictionary of Buddhism*, 330.

[37] Ibid., 130.

[38] Pema Chödrön, *When Things Fall Apart: Heart Advice for Difficult Times,* mass market ed. (Boston: Shambhala, 2005), 115–16.

Tonglen can be practiced to engage compassionately with the suffering of water. Take a moment and rest in meditation. Feel your mind open and expand. Now, visualize a polluted body of water. See the pollution vividly—plastic trash, a thick film of oil, dead fish and birds. Imagine that all of this pollution is condensing into a thick, black, hot smoke. As you breathe in, imagine that you take all this pollution into you. The smoke penetrates your heart, breaking it open, filling you with compassion. As you breathe out, exhale compassion in the form of a clear, light, white smoke. Breathing in, you breathe in all the pain and suffering of this water. Breathing out, you share your love with this water. Breathing in, you welcome all the suffering of water to enter into your body. Breathing out, you radiate peace, clarity, compassion.

As you meditate on polluted waters, you cultivate compassion, opening your heart and being with suffering, sharing love. *Tonglen* practice can be done at any time of the day. It can be done inside or outside, alone or in a group. *Tonglen* can help you become more empathetic with those who are suffering, including polluted bodies of water or marginalized people who do not have clean drinking water or improved sanitation.

This practice helps to generate a deep sense of compassion and helps to motivate us to liberate others from suffering.

CONCLUSION

The contemplative practices that I have described here are a brief selection of ways that can facilitate an integral water ethic. They focus on these general goals: paying attention and listening to the voices of water; cultivating intimacy with local, personal, and planetary waters; and embodying the cosmos by bringing water into one's consciousness and conscience. Drawing primarily from mindfulness and compassion exercises, these practices can help us "tune in" to the waters of our body and how they relate to the waters of the world.

We can practice living in communion with water and all our Earth community and thus cultivate mutually enhancing relations among humans, water, and the cosmos. Practices are important, because they address what we as individuals can do on a daily basis. Engaging in contemplative practices can be empowering, inspiring, and nourishing for our environmental efforts. With this attention to practices, I am focusing on ways to transform personal consciousness and behavior. By cultivating intimacy with water in our day-to-day life, we are able to transform our relationship with water and see water as a friend and teacher. This is the transformation we need in the Great Work of building mutually enhancing relations with our Earth community, becoming citizens of our Earth community who are working to create a flourishing future for all beings.

These are just a small sample of contemplative practices. Many other practices exist. For example, one could make a pilgrimage to sacred waters, engage mindfully in aquatic sports (swimming, surfing, kayaking, fishing),[39] meditate while soaking in a bathtub or hot tub, or create water music.[40] Given the infinite creativity of the human imagination, many practices are waiting to be developed. I invite you to consider ways in your own life that you can develop a more intimate connection with water. It is my hope that as we deepen our personal relationship with water, we will find practical ways of strengthening our commitment to be of service to our entire Earth community.

---

[39] Bron Taylor, "Focus Introduction: Aquatic Nature Religion," *Journal of the American Academy of Religion* 75, no. 4 (2007): 863–74.

[40] "Water music," as I am using it here, could include music with lyrics about water, music that imitates water, and music that incorporates water as an instrument.

Conclusion

Loving Water and All Beings

It is imperative that humans reinvent their relationship with water in light of the global water crisis. I have proposed an integral water ethic as a way for humans to cultivate a deeper sense of concern for the well-being of water and the Earth community. An integral water ethic is a way of interacting with water and all beings dependent upon water by cultivating values of love, compassion, respect, care, reverence, and gratitude. Such an ethic is situated in an integral approach to ecology and draws from perspectives from the world's religious traditions and contemplative practices. An integral water ethic considers water to be not merely a resource for human ends but a sacred source of life that has intrinsic value and its own interior dimension. To build a flourishing future for all beings, the many voices of water must be listened to and valued. An integral water ethic supports the cultivation of love and compassion for water and for all who suffer from the global water crisis; in doing so it promotes relating to water as a loving and compassionate being.

An integral water ethic holds that humans need to cultivate an I-Thou relationship with water.[1] Viewing water within an

---

[1] See Chapter 2 herein and Martin Buber, *I and Thou*, trans. Walter Kaufmann (New York: Touchstone, 1970).

I-It relationship would hold that water is an "It" and has only instrumental value for humans, not value in and of itself. Such a relationship views water as a mere resource, commodity, and sewer, and as a passive, inert substance with only objective dimensions. By cultivating an I-Thou relationship with water, humans would recognize that water is a "Thou" or "You" and has intrinsic value, not only instrumental value. This relationship would view water as a source of life, as a being that has some degree of interiority, and as a teacher and guide. Recalling the words of Larry Rasmussen, quoted in Chapter 2, "Water is the object of awe and not *only* the object of engineering; it is the medium of the mystical and not *only* a resource for a world of our own making; water is a 'thou' and not *only* an 'it.' . . . It's worthy of reverence."[2]

Drawing from the principle of cosmogenesis articulated by Brian Swimme and Thomas Berry, it is evident that water, like all beings in the cosmos, can be understood in terms of differentiation, autopoiesis, and communion.[3] Another way to say this is that water has objective, subjective, and relational dimensions. In other words, water has exteriority, interiority, and interrelatedness with other beings. Water is an integral being. As I discussed in Chapter 1, water's objective structure is articulated in its unique physical and chemical constitution that differentiates it from other beings in the cosmos. Water, like all beings in the universe, has some degree of interiority, which manifests as the self-organizing patterns of whirlpools, eddies, snowflakes, and waves. Water, as a complex being with objective and subjective dimensions, exists in interdependent relationality with all other beings in the Earth community.

---

[2] Larry L. Rasmussen, *Earth-honoring Faith: Religious Ethics in a New Key* (New York: Oxford University Press, 2013), 282.

[3] Brian Swimme and Thomas Berry, *The Universe Story: From the Primordial Flaring Forth to the Ecozoic Era—A Celebration of the Unfolding of the Cosmos* (San Francisco: HarperCollins, 1992), 71.

As an integral being, water is valued from the objective perspectives of the natural sciences and social sciences, as well as from the subjective perspectives of the humanities. I have highlighted the personal, cultural, and religious significance of water. Through exploring the traditions of Christianity, Hinduism, and Buddhism, I have considered three values that can contribute to an integral water ethic: sacramental consciousness, loving service, and compassionate wisdom. I have also explored how contemplative practices can further contribute to an integral water ethic by bringing into our conscious awareness and ethical concern the fact that water is of critical importance to all beings and deserves attention and care. Practices are important for an integral water ethic because they have the ability to help us cultivate a more intimate relationship with water by transforming our consciousness and conscience. One of my central points is that by practicing ways to love water and cultivate empathy and intimacy with water, we can extend our care for water to include all members of our Earth community. As a vital source of life, water connects us to all beings. By seeing water as an elemental thread that connects humans and the cosmos, we can cultivate empathy for all beings as we cultivate empathy for water.

In our day-to-day activities, we can practice developing a more intimate relationship with water and all members of our Earth community. We can practice having compassion, love, gratitude, and care for all bodies of water in our lives. By learning ways to cultivate an I-Thou relationship with water, we are able to embrace our role in the Great Work: to exist in mutually enhancing relations with all beings and dwell in communion with the cosmos in all its various manifestations. Recalling Thomas Berry's words, "The Great Work now, as we move into a new millennium, is to carry out the transition from a period of human devastation of the Earth to a period when humans would be present to the planet in a mutually beneficial manner."[4] This entails engaging in an active conversation with water and our whole world. As Berry notes:

> We have been treating the universe as a collection of objects. No matter how much these are interrelated with each other, if we do not hear the voices of the trees, the birds, the animals, the fish, the mountains and the rivers, then we are in trouble. . . . That, I think, is what has happened to the human community in our times. We are talking to ourselves. We are not talking to the river, we are not listening to the river. We have broken the great conversation. By breaking the conversation, we have shattered the universe.[5]

An integral water ethic is an attempt to enter into conversation with water. By listening to the many voices of water and the diverse perspectives of different cultures, we can work together to find more effective and integral ways to respond to the complexity of the global water crisis.

In our daily interactions with water we can have an intention to notice and pay attention. We can be attentive and responsive every time we drink water, bathe, or flush the toilet. We can notice water when we walk over a bridge. We can also notice when we do not see water as much, for example, when we experience a drought. We can pay attention to "virtual water," the hidden water that is involved in producing our food, clothes, shelters, medicines, modes of transportation, cell phones and computers, and more. For example, it takes approximately twenty-five hundred gallons of water to

---

[4] Thomas Berry, *The Great Work: Our Way into the Future* (New York: Random House, 1999), 3.

[5] Thomas Berry with Thomas Clark, *Befriending the Earth: A Theology of Reconciliation between Humans and the Earth*, ed. Stephen Dunn, CP, and Anne Lonergan (Mystic, CT: Twenty-Third Publications, 1991), 20.

produce one pound of coffee beans; eighteen hundred forty gallons of water for one pound of beef; and thirteen hundred gallons of water for one pound of cotton.[6] This is important to keep in mind for water conservation efforts. Noticing and paying attention are ways to practice having a water-drenched consciousness and conscience. In our daily lives we can learn to cultivate compassion and wisdom, practice loving service, and develop a sacramental consciousness. Water teaches us how to dwell intimately and empathetically with our world, to see the world as, in the words of Thomas Berry, "a communion of subjects, not a collection of objects."[7]

Through our daily interactions with water, we can learn to have a sense of cosmic regard. Neo-Confucian philosopher Zhang Zai (1020–1077) says it beautifully:

> Heaven is my father and Earth is my mother,
> and even such a small creature as I
> finds an intimate place in their midst.
> Therefore that which extends throughout
> the universe I regard as my body and
> that which directs the universe I con-
> sider as my nature.
> All people are my brothers and sisters, and
> all things are my companions.[8]

By practicing seeing water as a companion or kin, it is possible to expand this intimacy to include all beings. Furthermore,

---

[6] Tony Allan, *Virtual Water: Tackling the Threat to Our Planet* (London: I. B. Tauris and Co., 2011), 348.

[7] Thomas Berry, *Evening Thoughts: Reflecting on Earth as Sacred Community*, ed. Mary Evelyn Tucker (San Francisco: Sierra Club Books and University of California Press, 2006), 17.

[8] In William Theodore de Bary and Irene Bloom, eds., *Sources of Chinese Tradition: From Earliest Times to 1600*, 2nd ed. (New York: Columbia University Press, 1999), 1:683.

by paying attention to the prevalence of water throughout our own bodies, other living beings, and the hydrosphere, we can begin to see how the boundaries between humans and other beings are not clear and distinct but fluid. Humans are mostly water, just as other living beings are also mostly water. We are all aquatic bodies; we are all bodies of water. As such, we all intimately participate in the hydrological cycle. In a very real way humans are water seeing itself. We are bodies of water in human form who have the ability to become conscious of the fact that water is always flowing through us, that water is flowing as us. Just as we are the cosmos conscious of itself, we are water conscious of itself. As Berry says, "It is not that we think on the universe; the universe, rather, thinks *itself*, in us and through us."[9] Likewise, water thinks itself in us and through us.

WATER AS A TEACHER AND GUIDE
FOR AN INTEGRAL WATER ETHIC

An integral water ethic values the subjectivity of water, not only its objectivity. Recognizing that water has interiority, we can acknowledge that water can be a teacher and guide. In the chapters on Christianity, Hinduism, and Buddhism, I explored water in terms of sacramental consciousness, loving service, and compassionate wisdom.

As I explained in the chapter on Christianity, a sacramental consciousness of water helps us to recognize that all waters are blessed and sacred, a gift from God. Baptismal waters are a way to enter into communion with God. In this way water teaches an I-Thou relationship. By learning to see water in terms of "Thou," a being with intrinsic value, as opposed to an "It" that merely has instrumental value, we can learn to

---

[9] Berry, *Befriending the Earth*, 21.

see that all beings have intrinsic value and are part of a communion of subjects. The sacred character of water reflects the sacred character of all beings. Such a shift in consciousness has significant implications for social and environmental justice, for the poor and the marginalized are included in this communion of subjects. Jesus, who called himself Living Water, lived his life as an example of how to treat those who are marginalized. He said, "I was thirsty and you gave me something to drink. . . . Truly I tell you, just as you did it to one of the least of these who are members of my family, you did it to me" (Matt 25:35, 40). Manifesting acts of love for "the least of these" entails making sure that all beings have ample water to survive. This includes working toward clean drinking water and improved sanitation for all humans, as well as making sure that all members of the Earth community have the nourishing waters they need to flourish.

Cultivating loving service of water, as I explored in the chapter on Hinduism, can help us see water as a loving parent who serves its children, that is, all living beings. Water is a teacher of loving service, as it gives its waters freely to all. Recalling the words from Sunderlal Bahuguna:

> This river here flows for others. It is a model of loving service [*seva*]. Have you ever seen a river drinking its own water? Thus, nature sets an example for us human beings, and says that, if you want real peace and happiness, be in close contact with me. Living rivers give us so much.[10]

Krishna offers an example of loving service, as his love for Yamuna motivated him to tame the poisonous serpent Kaliya

---

[10] Sunderlal Bahuguna, in David L. Haberman, *River of Love in an Age of Pollution: The Yamuna River of Northern India* (Berkeley and Los Angeles: University of California Press, 2006), 72. Brackets in the original.

and restore health to the river. Krishna is an "ecological guru" who teaches us that all waters need our love and service.[11] This includes polluted rivers like the Yamuna, as well as polluted oceans, lakes, creeks, and estuaries.

As I noted in the Buddhism chapter, cultivating compassionate wisdom of water can enable us to see water as a compassionate and wise bodhisattva who nourishes all beings. Water teaches us the wisdom of the emptiness of any inherently existing self separate from the web of being. In light of this radical interdependence of all things, water teaches us how to compassionately respond to suffering, for the suffering of others is one's own suffering. The Seventeenth Karmapa is a helpful model for compassion and wisdom. As the embodiment of the bodhisattva Avalokiteśvara, the Karmapa founded the Khoryug network to teach ecological consciousness to Buddhist monks and nuns in the Himalayas. As he notes, the author of *The Way of the Bodhisattva* is a model for ecological wisdom: "If there were such a role as a Buddhist saint of ecology, I would nominate the great Indian scholar Shantideva."[12] The compassion and wisdom of the bodhisattva can be a guide for us to respond compassionately to the suffering that is widespread with the global water crisis. Through this example, we can learn to be with the suffering of others and work toward liberating them from suffering.

As we can see from these Christian, Hindu, and Buddhist examples, religious worldviews can teach us about the potential character of water's interiority. We can learn from the diverse perspectives of the world's religions to empathize with others, including water. What is the subjectivity

---

[11] Ibid., 155; see also Ranchor Prime, *Hinduism and Ecology: Seeds of Truth* (Delhi: Motilal Banarsidass Publishers, 1994), 54.

[12] His Holiness the Seventeenth Gyalwang Karmapa Ogyen Trinley Dorje, "Walking the Path of Environmental Buddhism through Compassion and Emptiness," *Conservation Biology* 25, no. 6 (2011): 1095.

of water? In asking this question, it is crucial to learn to see water as a teacher and to find ways to listen to the voices of water. Cultivating intimacy with water leads to a greater capacity for empathy.

The Great Work of our time provides us the opportunity to be of service to our Earth community. We are at a critical moment in history where we have the opportunity to be of service, to participate in the shift from a destructive, dominating attitude to a mutually enhancing relationship with water and all members of our Earth community. This crisis is an opportunity. How are we going to respond?

Cultivating an I-Thou relationship with water and our whole Earth community is key to the Great Work of our time. This is the task of an integral water ethic. It is imperative that humans transition out of the dominant way of viewing water (seeing water primarily as a resource, commodity, and sewer) and transition into a mutually enhancing relationship with water (seeing water as a teacher, a relative, a co-creator in the cosmic story of evolution). An integral water ethic is a way of life that aims to cultivate love and compassion for water and all our Earth community.

Water is life. Water connects all life. Water flows in a diversity of forms, including the forms of living beings. Life is animated water, as Vernadsky puts it.[13] If we can learn to see water as an elemental thread that connects all beings, then we can learn that cultivating intimacy and empathy with water helps us to have intimacy and empathy with all beings. Water is itself in relation to others. By understanding that, we can see that we humans are ourselves because of our relationships with others. We find ourselves enmeshed in a vibrant,

---

[13] In Stephan Harding and Lynn Margulis, "Water Gaia: 3.5 Thousand Million Years of Wetness on Planet Earth," in *Gaia in Turmoil: Climate Change, Biodepletion, and Earth Ethics in an Age of Crisis*, ed. Eileen Crist and H. Bruce Rinker (Cambridge, MA: MIT Press, 2010), 43.

complex web of relationships. The values of wisdom and compassion, loving service, and sacramental consciousness can assist us in the Great Work.

THE ROLE OF COMPREHENSIVE COMPASSION IN AN INTEGRAL WATER ETHIC

Water has the ability to teach us an integral water ethic. Water has the ability to help us fall in love with our entire Earth community and develop what Brian Swimme calls "comprehension compassion." In an interview in *What Is Enlightenment?* Swimme says that humans

> are the first species that actually has the possibility of caring about *all* of the other species. . . . The human being is that space in which the comprehensive compassion that pervades the universe from the very beginning now begins to surface *within consciousness*. That's the only difference. We didn't *invent* compassion, but it's flowing through us—or it could.[14]

We have the ability at this moment in cosmic evolution to care for species beyond our own. We can cultivate comprehensive compassion and become empathetic to all beings.

The notion of comprehensive compassion is further developed in *Journey of the Universe* by Swimme and Mary Evelyn Tucker. They explain that we are at a unique point in the evolution of the cosmos where we have the capacity to develop comprehensive compassion for all beings in the universe. We are the first species that is not concerned with caring only for our own species. We are a species that can now care for the whole cosmos. As Swimme and Tucker write:

---

[14] Brian Swimme, interview with Susan Bridle, "Comprehensive Compassion," *What Is Enlightenment?* 19 (Spring–Summer 2001): 7, 8.

The oceans too will be our guide as we journey into the future. The ocean is a power that can dissolve things into itself. Even the hardest rocks, given enough time, will become one with the ocean's waves.

With our symbolic consciousness, we are very much like the ocean with its power to pour through boundaries. What we long for is profound intimacy of relationship. Our human imagination brought something radically new to Earth's life: the capacity to experience the world from another's perspective. We call this empathy. What does this mean? In the mammalian world, a mother bear has the capacity to identify with her young cubs and thus devote herself to their well-being. With the emergence of humans, we have arrived at an evolutionary breakthrough for being able to develop compassion, not just for our offspring, but for all beings of every order of existence. With this alone, Earth gave rise to the possibility of an empathetic being who could flow into and become one with the intimate feelings of any being.

Our human destiny is to become the heart of the universe that embraces the whole of the Earth community. We are just a speck in the universe, but we are beings with the capacity to feel comprehensive compassion in the midst of an ocean of intimacy. That is the direction of our becoming more fully human.[15]

As the above passage notes, humans are like the ocean in our capacity for empathetic love. Water teaches us how to love, how to dissolve boundaries and flow into the feelings of another. At this time in cosmic evolution we have this opportunity to open up our hearts and minds and step into our

---

[15] Brian Swimme and Mary Evelyn Tucker, *Journey of the Universe* (New Haven, CT: Yale University Press, 2011), 115.

role here in this universe, to become the heart and mind of the cosmos. We have the capacity to learn to love all things in the universe. Water is our guide.

Tu Weiming's idea that humans can embody the cosmos in our consciousness and conscience is important here: "The uniqueness of being human is the intrinsic capacity of the mind to 'embody' *(t'i)* the cosmos in its conscience and consciousness. Through this embodying, the mind realizes its own sensitivity, manifests true humanity and assists in the cosmic transformation of Heaven and Earth."[16] Because we have this ability to embody the cosmos in our heart and mind, we ought to practice it. We can do this through practicing the values of an integral water ethic.

The religions of the world and the story of the universe help us see water as a gift, a gift from God, a gift from the cosmos. Water is a unique part of creation stories and plays a unique role in the story of evolution. It is important for us to learn to care for water, to open our hearts to this gift of life, and to give gratitude. Giving thanks and having care—that is what we are being called to do in our Great Work. Loving water is a way to love God. Loving water is a way to love all of creation, to love the whole universe. As Thich Nhat Hanh writes: "Through my love for you, I want to express my love for the whole cosmos, the whole of humanity, and all beings. By living with you, I want to learn to love everyone and all species. If I succeed in loving you, I will be able to love everyone and all species on Earth."[17] By learning to love one thing deeply, we can learn to love all things. By loving one body of water, we can love all bodies of water and all beings in the cosmos.

---

[16] Tu Weiming, *Confucian Thought: Selfhood as Creative Transformation*, SUNY Series in Philosophy (Albany: State University of New York Press, 1985), 132.

[17] Thich Nhat Hanh, *Teachings on Love* (Berkeley, CA: Parallax Press, 1998), 98.

We can learn how to have a loving relationship with water, one of humility, gratitude, care, openness—an openness to the mystery of water, the mystery of God, the mystery of all things in the cosmos. Water can teach us how to do this. By cultivating intimacy with water, humans can feel a deep connection with the cosmos. Water is a unique, precious, sacred element, and by opening our hearts to this element, we can learn to open our hearts and bear witness to the mystery of all things.

LOOKING AHEAD TO FUTURE RESEARCH

As I noted in the Introduction, this book is not an attempt to be a definitive account of an integral water ethic but instead one particular contribution to such an ethic. I look forward to seeing alternative contributions to an integral water ethic in the future. For instance, further research is needed to explore other religious traditions to investigate their unique contributions to an integral water ethic. I think indigenous traditions throughout the world would especially have much to offer for an integral water ethic, particularly in terms of the personhood of water and the value of gratitude.

In the future it would also be valuable to investigate how an integral water ethic could contribute to issues of social justice, policy decisions, economics, and watershed management. An integral water ethic would value the many different perspectives related to particular bodies of water, including those perspectives that are often marginalized and neglected, such as those of the poor, minorities, and women. As such, an integral water ethic constitutes a democratic approach to watershed management, economics, and policy, working toward water justice and peace.

Furthermore, future research would have much to explore in terms of the role of art for an integral water ethic. Artistic expressions through poetry, music, dance, painting, and sculpture are ways to connect personal experiences with local and global waters. One example of an endeavor focusing on water is River of Words. Founded by US poet laureate Robert Hass and the watershed activist Pamela Michael, River of Words was created in 1995 as an international K–12 program that encourages youth to explore the natural and cultural history of the watersheds where they live and to create poetry and paintings based on their experiences.[18] As Michael reflects, "We soon began defining our mission as 'helping children fall in love with the earth.' Because people protect what they love, this is a powerful prescription for stewardship, and ultimately, we hope, kinship."[19] Art has the ability to connect the heart and the mind and can act as a powerful and transformative medium for an integral water ethic.

THE ART OF LOVING WATER

Love is at the heart of transforming our relationship with water and the world. Love is key to an integral water ethic. As Thich Nhat Hanh writes:

> We have to learn the art of loving. Love by the way you walk, the way you sit, the way you eat. . . . I am more and more convinced that the next Buddha may not be just one person, but he may be a community, a community of love. We need to support each other to build a community where love is something tangible. This may be the most important thing we can do for the survival

---

[18] Pamela Michael, "Helping Children Fall in Love with the Earth: Environmental Education and the Arts," in *Ecological Literacy: Educating Our Children for a Sustainable World*, ed. Michael K. Stone and Zenobia Barlow (San Francisco: Sierra Club Books, 2005), 112.

[19] Ibid., 116.

of the Earth. We have everything except love. We have to renew our way of loving. We have to really learn to love. The well-being of the world depends on us, on the way we live our daily lives, on the way we take care of the world, and on the way we love.[20]

Likewise, the well-being of water depends on the way that we love and care for water. The art of loving water is something that each of us can learn how to do in our own way. Every person can play his or her unique role in the Great Work of creating mutually enhancing relations with water and all beings. Every voice matters, just as every drop of water matters. As the Seventeenth Karmapa reflects: "The challenge of environmental degradation is far more complex and extensive than anything we alone can tackle. However, if we can all contribute a single drop of clean water, those drops will accumulate into a fresh pond, then a clear stream and eventually a vast pure ocean. This is my aspiration."[21] If each of us can contribute to the work of cultivating an integral water ethic, our individual efforts will combine to something much larger than any one of us could dream.

Osprey Orielle Lake, the executive director of the Women's Earth and Climate Action Network, tells a story of visiting a creek that was special to her and finding that it had stopped flowing due to heavy silt from a timber operation. When she saw the irreversible damage caused to the creek, something changed within her.

I lay down in the meadow, and the entire mountain seemed to grieve with me. I pledged in that moment to

---

[20] Nhat Hanh, *Teachings on Love,* 141.

[21] His Holiness the Seventeenth Gyalwang Karmapa Ogyen Trinley Dorje, *Environmental Guidelines for Kagyu Buddhist Monasteries, Centers and Community* (Archana, New Delhi: Archana Press, 2008), 2.

give my voice to the creek, to the waters. . . . There are a hundred thousand ways to do this, and each person can find his or her own way that stirs personal passion, from water justice campaigns to watershed restoration projects, from education to the arts. Each voice is a rivulet adding to the river of necessary life-sustaining power and momentum capable of changing the course of our human relationship to water. Every drop counts. Every contribution to the combined flow of change for the better is valuable.[22]

Each of our unique voices matters. Ocean explorer and activist Liz Cunningham notes that one of the guiding questions in her life is this: "What if I lived as if my voice mattered?"[23] There are innumerable ways that we can share our voice with the world. When we align our actions with what we most love to do, our work is nourished by our love and is better able to sustain hardships along the way.

Sandra Steingraber, an ecologist and environmental justice activist, writes that the environmental crisis can be addressed most effectively if we all find our unique passions and do what we do best to the best of our ability:

But rather than give in to despair, the answer, I think, is to pick one part of the problem about which you already have expertise and passion and work as hard as you can on that single piece.

If you are a musician, let me put it this way: It is time to play the *Save the World* symphony. It is a vast

---

[22] Osprey Orielle Lake, *Uprisings for the Earth: Reconnecting Culture with Nature* (Ashland, OR: White Cloud Press, 2010), 193–94.

[23] Liz Cunningham, *Ocean Country: One Woman's Voyage from Peril to Hope in Her Quest to Save the Seas* (Berkeley, CA: North Atlantic Books, 2015), 270.

orchestral piece, and you are but one musician. You are not required to play a solo, but you are required to figure out what your instrument is and play it as well as you can.[24]

Reflecting on this quotation, environmental philosopher Kathleen Dean Moore notes that "there is no score. No one has written the Save the World Symphony. We're making it up as we go along. This is not classical music. This is jazz, with all its risk and glory."[25] Improvisation is a skill we need to practice as we respond to the emerging complexities of the global water crisis. Moore reminds us of ways that water can help us recharge and renew our love of the world:

> Let the reliable rhythms of the moon and the tides reassure you. Let the smells return memories of other seas and times. Let the reflecting light magnify your perception. Let the rhythm of the rushing water flood your spirit. Walk and walk until your heart is full. Then you will remember why you try so hard to protect this beloved world, and why you must.[26]

Robin Wall Kimmerer, a professor of environmental biology at the State University of New York College of Environmental Science and Forestry and a member of the Citizen Band Potawatomi, explains that the Earth calls us to give our gifts: "What does the Earth ask of us? To meet our responsibilities and to give our gifts. . . . So when we ask ourselves,

---

[24] Sandra Steingraber, "Living Downstream from *Silent Spring*," in *Rachel Carson: Legacy and Challenge*, ed. Lisa H. Sideris and Kathleen Dean Moore (Albany: State University of New York Press, 2008), 228.

[25] Kathleen Dean Moore, *Great Tide Rising: Toward Clarity and Moral Courage in a Time of Climate Change* (Berkeley, CA: Counterpoint, 2016), 305.

[26] Ibid., 267.

what is our responsibility to the Earth, we are also asking 'What is our gift?'"[27]

By practicing our own unique ways of loving water, of embodying water in our consciousness and conscience, we can take up our role in the Great Work and work toward a flourishing future for the Earth community. How can we learn to love water more deeply? Practice is key. We can practice cultivating an integral water ethic by forming an intimate love for the local waters we interact with on a daily basis. We can then practice extending that love to encompass comprehensive compassion for all beings. By learning to love one thing deeply, we can learn to love all things deeply. By developing intimacy with a particular lake, creek, or river, we can open our hearts to love. When we experience the depths of love, we can see how love is able to extend out to all beings. Water helps us connect to our whole Earth community. The oceans teach us empathy and comprehensive compassion. Water is a guide for learning how to love our Earth community.

An integral water ethic is a way to relate to water so that we can extend our concern to all beings in the cosmos. By learning to cultivate compassion in our day-to-day lives, in our own spheres of influence, we can learn how to open our hearts and listen to the voices of water, to the voices of all beings, so that we might learn how to become responsible and compassionate members of our local watersheds, the Earth community, and the cosmic community.

Listening to water as a source of inspiration can help in the Great Work to create a flourishing future for all beings.

This is our Great Work: to listen to the voice of the river.

---

[27] Robin Wall Kimmerer, "Returning the Gift," *Minding Nature* 7, no. 2 (2014): 23.

This is our Great Work: to cultivate an intimacy with our world.

This is our Great Work: to become activists and advocates for water and all beings.

This is our Great Work: to see ourselves in relation to the cosmos and cultivate mutually enhancing relations between water and our Earth community.

How can we cultivate love and compassion for water, this sacred source of life? May this question continue resounding in our ears, so that we might hear it over and over as the mantra of the Great Work. May we return to this question again and again and ask water to teach us how to love our world and all beings in our Earth community. May we ask with our full being, with every breath, with every step, with every sip of water.

Index